Evolutionary
Jurisprudence

Evolutionary Jurisprudence

*Prospects and Limitations
on the Use of Modern Darwinism
throughout the Legal Process*

John H. Beckstrom

University of Illinois Press
Urbana and Chicago

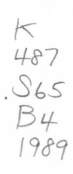
© 1989 by the Board of Trustees of the University of Illinois
Manufactured in the United States of America
C 5 4 3 2 1

This book is printed on acid-free paper.

Library of Congress Cataloging-in-Publication Data

Beckstrom, John H., 1932-
    Evolutionary jurisprudence : prospects and limitations on the use of
modern Darwinism throughout the legal process / John H. Beckstrom.
        p.   cm.
    Bibliography: p.
    Includes index.
    ISBN 0-252-01621-1 (alk. paper)
    1. Law and sociobiology. I. Title.
K487.S65B4   1989
344'.095—dc19
[342.495]   88-32112
                                                         CIP

Contents

Acknowledgments

I wish to thank the following people for reading and commenting on early versions of various parts of this book: Ian Ayres, Blake Beckstrom, Robert W. Bennett, Beth Bower, Martin Daly, Anthony D'Amato, Richard Dawkins, John Donohue, Mark Flinn, Clinton Francis, Harry D. Krause, Edward Lev, Roger D. Masters, John B. Oakley, Richard A. Posner, Lawrence Rosen, Robert Trivers, Pierre L. van den Berghe, Edward O. Wilson, and Margo Wilson.

Northwestern University's School of Law and Harvard University's Museum of Comparative Zoology provided resources and colleagues enabling me to develop the content of this book.

Introduction

This book deals with interrelationships of law and scientific learning concerning human behavior. The scientific learning it discusses is an emerging synthesis — an amalgam of developing fact and theory that has been variously labeled. It is most often called human sociobiology, a name that impressed itself on the public consciousness in the mid-1970s, when the subject first received popular media attention. Other terms used by theorists and empiricists in the field have been evolutionary biology, evolution and human behavior, and just plain Darwinism (in recognition of the principal contributor to the field). No one term has been completely satisfactory, because it was either too broad or too narrow to encompass the field and the scientists in it. Developments in recent years have suggested that a good name for the field might be biocultural science. Nevertheless, human sociobiology (or just sociobiology when the "human" is understood from the context) has tenaciously hung on as the most often used label for the discipline. That should be acceptable as long as one keeps in mind that this scientific discipline has come a long way since its public exposure in the mid-1970s: a host of leading scientists are currently working in the area, building on foundations established by countless scientists of the past.

Since sociobiology deals with the social behavior of all organisms, including humans, and since the law regulates and otherwise deals with human behavior, it was inevitable that sociobiologists and lawyers would find common ground. Efforts to investigate that ground have come from both sides but have been hampered by the fact that few natural scientists are well versed in the law and few lawyers have natural-science backgrounds. Unfortunately, neither the relevant law nor the relevant science can be learned in a weekend short-course.

Since most laypeople have a general grasp of legal concepts, I am confident that I can introduce the relevant details of the law without providing an initial general introduction to the law. That is not the case with the relevant science, however, because it involves factual discoveries and theoretical developments with which most laypeople are unfamiliar except perhaps in some vague or intuitive sense. Therefore, I begin the book with a chapter containing an introductory overview of sociobiology; other biocultural and natural history facts and theories are introduced as the book progresses. (In addition, I cite authorities in numbered notes at the end of each chapter; these notes often contain substantive incidental comments and supportive quotations.)

One of my purposes in this book is to encourage natural scientists and lawyers to spend the time necessary to learn what is relevant in each others' areas. Thus the primary readers I have targeted are lawyers and natural scientists. But I hope the book will reach social scientists as well. To accommodate both lawyers and natural scientists, I have presented both the science and the law in lay language, which I believe makes the presentation intelligible to others, such as social scientists, who are trained in neither the natural sciences nor the law.

In my earlier book, *Sociobiology and the Law*, I opted to use an anthropomorphic language device: rather than detailing the evolutionary process that is said to bear on human behavior, I asked the reader to assume that genes were "urging" their carriers toward certain behaviors or "whispering" to them. This device has the virtue of holding a larger reading audience than a technical presentation, but it invites suspicion that one is being drawn into some kind of spiritualistic seance rather than a scientific study.

In this book I will be a bit more technical. I will still frequently use the term "programming" to refer to the way in which genetic makeup is said to interact with the environment and culture to produce human behavior, but I will first explain why such a mildly anthropomorphic term may be justified. I encourage the uninitiated reader to turn for more detail to a large array of written sources and not draw any conclusions about sociobiology until then.[1] Here I will assume that the discipline is generally on the mark about human behavior and then explore the potential the discipline holds for assisting the law and lawmakers if its assumptions are correct. A major part of that potential revolves around human aid-giving behavior, so my discussion of sociobiology will pay particular attention to that topic. *Sociobiology and the Law* had that as its main focus also. However, this book is intended to cover new ground, such as exploring limitations on the use of sociobiology. Although *Sociobiology and the Law* dealt with material on the use of sociobiology in the legal process that is only alluded to in this book, one need not have read the earlier work as a prelude to this one. (In fact, if one is inclined to read both, I recommend that this one be read first.)

Those who take the time to understand the overlap of disciplines explored in this book should find it well worth the effort: the potential for sociobiology and the law to gain from each other is very impressive. If and when sociobiological theory becomes well settled and substantiated, it could be used in various ways in the legal process. Although that potential is explored throughout the book, it belongs to the long run—there are more immediate possibilities for fruitful cross-fertilization between sociobiology and the law.

In particular, legal sources might be used to test sociobiology. Sociobiological theory concerning human behavior is presently being empirically tested in several arenas, but to date no one has utilized the vast resource of commentaries on human behavior, dating back over three hundred years, held by law libraries. The potential of this resource is the subject of the last chapter of this book.

In addition, there is immediate potential for a unique type of mutually beneficial cooperative empirical research to be conducted by lawyers and scientists in areas where their concerns regarding typical human behavior overlap. Such research could produce data of use to lawmakers while simultaneously testing scientists' behavioral hypotheses. This is the focus of chapter II.

The natural science that sociobiology synthesizes may become an important aid one day in helping people to better understand themselves and solve their problems—including problems presented to judges, legislators, and other officials who make rules (hereafter referred to collectively as "lawmakers"). But no one would suppose that sociobiology could be used to help solve every problem that exists in the legal process. While outlining ways in which it could be used, I will also explore limitations on its use. That subject is treated in chapters III and V.

Lawmakers have developed official viewpoints on facts about human nature important to the legal process, and natural scientists search for such facts in a systematic way—but both lawmakers and scientists are subject to perceptual biases when they theorize about, search for, locate, and report these facts. I ask the reader to join me in assessing the correctness of what lawmakers and natural scientists report about human nature by adjusting for possible bias in the reports and attempting to eliminate our own personal and political biases when making our assessments.

Some have viewed sociobiology as providing support for ideological or political positions. Politics, of course, infuse the lawmaking process. Lawmakers may, therefore, be curious as to whether sociobiology can help resolve public debates by pointing to societal goals that ought to be promoted through the legal process. In chapter III, I explain why sociobiology appears to be of no value in that regard, while having definite potential for mechanically *facilitating* the achievement of goals that have been otherwise selected. However, I will demonstrate a *nonpartisan* political use of sociobiology in chapter VI. I will show how sociobiological concepts could be used to critique the performance of incumbent lawmakers in any established regime that purports to represent the best interests of a constituency, whether that regime is labeled conservative, liberal, or middle of the road.

I believe that the reader will be able to conclude with me that the potential value of sociobiology to the legal process does not lie in supporting any incumbent regime or any advocate's view of what society ought to be like. The potential value to the legal process rests elsewhere—in instructing all of us, whatever side we may take on debated issues and whether we are in or out of the government, on the *facts* of natural history that bear on the predictability of human behavior when knowledge of such predictability is important to the resolution of social problems.

What is my position in all this? For thirty-three years I have been a student of the law, though the majority of my study time in the past decade has been in the natural sciences. However, I do not consider myself either a lawyer or a scientist. I am a reporter—reporting on the common ground that exists between a body of science and the law. I personally applaud both lawyers and natural scientists for their efforts to discover facts about human behavior, and I would like to demonstrate ways in which they might assist each other in those efforts.

NOTES

1. A good initial program would include study of the following sources in the order indicated: Dawkins, *The Selfish Gene*; chapters 1, 2, and 3 of Barash, *The Hare and the Tortoise*; Trivers, *Social Evolution*; Alexander, *Darwinism and Human Affairs*; Lumsden and Wilson, *Promethean Fire*.

Chapter

I

Sociobiology: The Nature and Nurture Mix of Human Behavior

Sociobiology is complicated. It blends recent natural science theories and discoveries with the earlier work of Charles Darwin, Gregor Mendel, and many others. It includes elements drawn from evolutionary biology, population genetics, anthropology, ethology, and other related disciplines. A prominent scientist has recently warned that the science involved cannot be learned from any one book.[1] Instead, extensive reading of various sources is required. This state of affairs creates a problem, to say the least, for one attempting to introduce the subject in a short space as a prelude to relating it to a field like the law.

In this overview, I will describe what I take to be the consensus thinking of sociobiologists. Despite accumulating empirical support for that thinking, little of it can presently be stated as fact; nevertheless, I will state the sociobiological position here without resorting to cumbersome qualifying clauses in each sentence. Thus, for example, I may say that "humans are inclined to render aid to close relatives before strangers" rather than "there is accumulating empirical support for the sociobiological hypothesis that evolutionary processes have resulted in humans typically aiding close genetic and in-law relatives before comparative strangers, everything else being equal."

We could begin our story with the cosmic "big bang" or, later in time, with the primordial ooze from which it is thought that life on earth emerged. But as this book deals with human beings, we will skip ahead to early human history. In that setting, let us begin by illustrating the concept contained in the term natural selection, which refers to a key process in the evolutionary history of all organisms, including humans.[2] That process has been one in which individuals with certain

genetically influenced characteristics have tended to survive and reproduce more successfully than others without such characteristics.[3]
The exact details of our early evolutionary history cannot be known,
but one can assume plausible scenarios that illustrate the process.

For example, an early ancestor of ours could have carried a gene
(more likely a combination of genetic materials,[4] but let us assume a
single gene), developed by mutation, that gave her the dexterity and
insight to use some simple tool, such as a sharp stone, found in her
environment. This capacity resulted in her surviving during hard times
while others around her who were not thus genetically endowed were
dying off. Because she prospered longer than others, she produced
more offspring. A large percentage of those offspring inherited that
special gene so they, in turn, were more successful in staying alive and
reproducing than were others around them. Eventually, after a great
many generations had passed, essentially every human alive carried
this gene. This happened because those who did not carry the gene
were at a competitive disadvantage in dealing with adverse environments. They therefore had been slowly washed out of the "gene pool"
that represents the total combined genetic complement of a population
at any given time.

In the above scenario, the behavioral characteristics that the special gene promoted were being *selected* by the natural process. Indeed,
the gene itself was being selected; selection was acting at the level of
the gene. The gene was surviving from generation to generation because
it was "fit"; it was only incidental that the individuals who carried it
had high survival value and were relatively "fit" in terms of reproductive capacity.[5] This is an evolutionary insight that modern science
has provided.[6] Darwin knew something survived as represented in the
term "survival of the fittest," but he was unclear as to exactly what it
was. Genes, as well as the chromosomes upon which they are found
and the DNA of which they are composed, were there, but undiscov-
ered in his day.

Evolution is, of course, a continuing process. As the environments
of our ancestors have changed and increased through the ages, vast
numbers of genes or combinations of genetic materials bearing on
behavioral traits that adapted well to varying environments have arisen
and settled into the gene pool that represents all humans living today.
We are thus all quite well "programmed" to survive and reproduce in
the environments in which we find ourselves. Some behavior in response to the environment is "hard-wired" genetically (relatively inflexible) like eye blinking. Blinking moistens and helps clear the surface
of the eye as air and dust come into contact with it. No great advantage

would have accrued to a genetic program that promoted complex calculation or thought before blinking, so any such neurologically expensive program that popped up in the gene pool by mutation would have been selected against by the economics of nature.[7] Other behavior is quite loosely programmed; this is because flexibility has often had survival and reproductive value, since it permits adjustment to rapid and diverse changes in unpredictable environments. As wind, rain, snow, disease-causing organisms, predators, and competitors have appeared and disappeared, those who could respond most flexibly were often better adapted. And it has been advantageous for individuals to be able to learn by trial and error how best to respond to a given environmental circumstance. Programming for this type of learning capacity has thus been selected for in the evolutionary process leading to today's human beings. Thus the genetic programming that permitted that remote ancestor to remember and reapply the skill of using a sharp stone as a tool was retained and proliferated in the gene pool.

Now, theoretically, sharp stone use might have spread in the population by the tedious route of each individual stumbling onto it by trial and error. Most certainly it did not happen that way. Instead, people in whom genetic programming developed that permitted them to learn by observing and imitating (sharp stone use, fire use, warm clothing use, the use of the wheel—and the use of books) had an advantage on an advantage, as it were. Thus vicarious, as well as firsthand, learning capacity proliferated in the gene pool.

Notice that with vicarious learning, culture entered into the human picture. Useful devices for survival and reproduction could now be passed rapidly, in a moment's time, from person to person without having to wait for the lockstep, generation-to-generation reproductive process by which genes and genetic programming are inherited. But keep in mind that the *capacity* to learn from accumulated culture is genetically programmed. And that capacity, *at any given moment in evolutionary time*, has had outward limits. At present, for example, starting with mother's milk, we can go on to learn to ingest hamburgers, artichokes, and red hot peppers. (I once followed someone's example by eating a pigeon's head in Malaysia and could do it again if need be.) However, if seed salespeople were to promote lawn grass as food, very few, if any, of us could "learn" that. Unlike sheep, we cannot adequately digest and gain nutrition from grass.

By putting a minimum of two people in our picture (one to learn from the other), we have also moved into the social dimension of human life—let us stay there. Picture a crowd and then focus on one individual. That individual (a gene carrier) has a package of evolved genetic material that programs the carrier well to compete with others for life-sustaining resources and reproductive opportunities. Gene shuffling during the sexual reproduction process[8] assures that the gene carrier's package is unique (unless the carrier has an identical twin). From this fact one might assume that people would be programmed always to act to promote the survival and reproduction of their own particular genetic package. Indeed, sociobiology holds this as a basic tenet. How, then, can one account for aid-giving between individuals? Here sociobiology has provided theoretical insights that have been admired even by some of the discipline's most noted critics.[9]

Any gene one person carries (aside from rare aberrations)[10] is and has been carried by other individuals as well. Each carrier has an identical copy of the gene. Wherever a gene appears it is identical in each incarnation, and all copies of a gene are of equal value to the genetic material they represent. There is a key concept here that must be appreciated if the rest of evolutionary biology is to be understood. It is extremely useful to employ an anthropomorphic device to convey this concept, so pardon me while I do: any gene you contain is equally as "interested" in its copy in another person as it is in itself. A genetic mechanism, whether due to one gene or a combination, that promotes aid-giving could, therefore, be selected in the evolutionary process. This would happen when any loss in reproductive capacity (fitness) to the aid-giver is sufficiently offset by a gain in fitness to others containing high percentages of the same genetic material. I will illustrate this with a frequently used simplified example involving sibling rescue.[11] But let me lead into the example with a word about genetic overlap between close relatives.

In order to express the genetic overlap of close relatives in a telegraphic manner, one might say, for example, that siblings have a 50-percent overlap. Technically, however, the total genetic overlap of even the most distant relatives is much larger. *All* humans alive today share, in common, the vast majority of their genes. But over and above those genes that prevail in the entire species, there is additional gene commonality between close relatives. You and your siblings, on the average, share 50 percent of these "familial" genes by inheritance from your parents.[12]

Now, assume you find yourself in a situation where you could either save yourself or three of your siblings. If you save yourself and let your siblings die, you have saved 100 percent of your familial gene copies. Remember, however, that all copies of a gene are of equal value to the genetic material they represent. Thus if you sacrifice yourself and save your three siblings, you have saved about 150 percent of the genetic material represented in your copies of your familial genes. The siblings, combined, would be in a better position to reproduce that genetic material than you alone would be. For these reasons sociobiologists suggest that any genetic programming prompting self-sacrifice for three siblings would have a reproductive advantage and would therefore proliferate in the gene pool. Sociobiologists assume that aid-giving tendencies of this sort were *selected* in humans ages ago and exist in us today. The phenomenon, first elaborated by W. D. Hamilton, is called *kin selection* by natural scientists, and its existence in nature has been substantiated—in particular, by elegant experiments with social insects.[13]

The evolutionary calculus of aid-giving is much more complicated than indicated by our sibling-saving example. For instance, if your siblings were beyond reproductive age and you were still within it, the calculations that you would be assumed to make, unconsciously at least, would ease the balance toward your favor. But, *everything else being equal*, sociobiologists would predict that you would sacrifice yourself for your three siblings because of the high percentage of familial genes you share in common with them.

The genetic relatedness between relatives is expressed by geneticists in terms of fractions, like one-half for siblings. In the computation of these fractional relationships the focus is on the "familial" genes mentioned above—that is, genes that are common within a family but comparatively rare in the population as a whole.[14] The fraction for parent and offspring is always one-half: you have one-half of your mother's genes and one-half of your father's genes. For all other relationships the figure represents an average. If you had 100 brothers and sisters, approximately 50 of them would contain less than half of your familial genes and 50 of them more than half, for an average of one-half. Similarly, half-siblings are related by one-fourth, as are grandparents and grandchildren and the aunt/uncle–niece/nephew combinations. Cousins are related by one-eighth. A family tree showing genetic relatedness is set out in the figure on p. 10.

The effects of kin selection on aid-giving behavior are manifested in countless everyday settings short of the extreme "save your siblings" example we have used. Assume I have an indivisible piece of a life-sustaining resource that I do not presently need and several people surrounding me are in need of it. These people are related to me in varying degrees. Sociobiologists would predict, everything else being equal, that, if I give it away, I would give it to my child before I would give it to my niece, since my children (one-half–related) would, when mating with people unrelated to me, reproduce an average of one-

The Family Tree

(The fractions after each group of relatives indicate the degree of genetic relatedness of anyone in that group to Ego.)

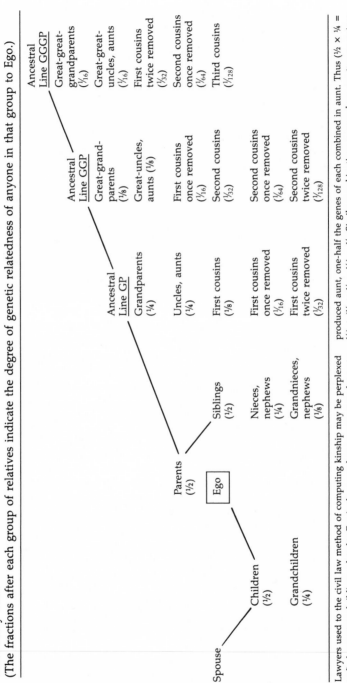

	Ancestral Line GP	Ancestral Line GGP	Ancestral Line GGGP
			Great-great-grandparents (1/16)
		Great-grandparents (1/8)	Great-great-uncles, aunts (1/16)
Parents (1/2)	Grandparents (1/4)	Great-uncles, aunts (1/8)	First cousins twice removed (1/32)
Siblings (1/2)	Uncles, aunts (1/4)	First cousins once removed (1/16)	Second cousins once removed (1/64)
Nieces, nephews (1/4)	First cousins (1/8)	Second cousins (1/32)	Third cousins (1/128)
Grandnieces, nephews (1/8)	First cousins once removed (1/16)	Second cousins once removed (1/64)	
	First cousins twice removed (1/32)	Second cousins twice removed (1/128)	

Ego | Spouse

Children (1/2)

Grandchildren (1/4)

Lawyers used to the civil law method of computing kinship may be perplexed to find parents and siblings related to Ego in the same degree, as are grandparents and uncles/aunts. In the civil law method one counts up from Ego to the common ancestor, then down to the kin in question. This results, e.g., in aunts being considered, legally, as more remote "blood" kin than grandparents, though genetically they are the same degree distant. The genetic explanation is this: both grandparents are ancestors related to Ego by 1/4. When they together produced aunt, one-half the genes of each combined in aunt. Thus (1/2 × 1/4 = 1/8) + (1/2 × 1/4 = 1/8) = 1/4. Similar combinations occur when any two ancestors mate together, as when Ego's parents produced his siblings. When a relative mates with a (comparative) genetic stranger, the result is different. E.g., when aunt (related by 1/4) mates with a man unrelated to Ego, the genes of Ego found in the resulting cousin include one-half the familial genes aunt has in common with Ego. Thus cousin and Ego are related by 1/8.

fourth of my familial genes in each grandchild (½ of ½ = ¼), whereas my nieces (one-fourth–related) would reproduce an average of only one-eighth of those genes (½ of ¼ = ⅛) in each offspring. Similarly, sociobiologists predict, all else being equal, I would aid my niece before my cousin, whose children would only have roughly one-sixteenth of my familial genes (½ of ⅛ = ¹⁄₁₆). My cousin, however, would get my aid before a comparative stranger would.

But why do we aid strangers at all if natural selection has programmed each of us to act for the benefit of the gene package we carry? Here is where a second modern theoretical insight bearing on sociality comes into the picture. It is usually called *reciprocal altruism*.[15]

The principle of reciprocal altruism assumes that evolutionary processes have selected for genetic programming that promotes aid-giving under circumstances where an aid-giver has reasonable assurance that there will eventually be at least a substantively equivalent return for the benefit of his or her genetic material. Thus it is assumed that any genetic programming would be selected for if it promoted the giving of life-sustaining aid by *A* to *B* when the cost to *A* is slight compared to *B*'s need and the likelihood is high that *B* would return the favor under similar circumstances. The forms of reciprocal altruism can be varied and complex—the key is that natural selection has favored reciprocal social behavior that promoted the reproduction of an individual's genetic complement. Returns for aid given may be experienced in the short or long run and may be experienced by persons other than the aid-giver, such as children, grandchildren, or nieces and nephews who contain high degrees of genetic overlap with the aid-giver.

Commercial life insurance is a somewhat complex manifestation of the reciprocal altruism principle. In the life insurance scheme, one pays an amount of money into a fund that will benefit strangers. However, there is a good chance that a larger amount will someday, on the death of the insured, be paid out of the fund to (usually) people who are in a good position to promote the continuance and proliferation in the population gene pool of representatives of the insured's gene package. The capacity to enter into all such arrangements may well have genetic underpinnings in that we have the ability to learn and utilize them when they are within the range of alternatives that promote the survival and reproduction of our genetic material.[16]

With all this discussion of genetic programming, we should not lose sight of the cultural input to human behavior. I mentioned rudimentary culture earlier when discussing our remote ancestors and the evolution of our ability to learn from our environment. Culture surrounds us, of course, today in all its complex multidimensional manifestations, ready to be learned and applied (as appropriate) in the pursuit of survival and reproduction. The commercial life insurance I just mentioned is a fairly complex cultural creation; so are mousetraps, representative government, the refrigerator, Zen Buddhism, child-care centers, and the Australian crawl stroke. They are there waiting to be learned and applied to the extent that our genetic programming permits.

What about the issue of whether our behavior is caused by genes *or* culture—or, as it was more popularly known, the nature-nurture debate? Among scientists the issue no longer exists in an either/or form. It is fair to say that no serious scientist any longer believes that all human behavior is completely attributable to acculturation. Nor does any scientist today believe (if any ever did) that all human behavior is completely attributable to genetic programming. The issues now (largely empirical questions) are the ways and degrees to which genetic programming and culture intermix with respect to particular aspects of our behavior. These issues await resolution by social and natural scientists.[17]

What sociobiology offers is a new way of looking at human behavior. It sees behavior varying from society to society as environments and cultures vary, because our behavior results from the interaction of relatively constant genetically programmed predispositions and the more volatile natural, social, and cultural environments we encounter. We human gene carriers are programmed to head toward a definite ultimate goal—optimum proliferation of our genetic package—and we must bounce off, adjust to, and utilize what we encounter in our particular environments as we head toward that goal. Let me bring that high-flown metaphor down to a focus that is important for the subject of this book.

Our aid-giving behavior will vary depending on things like the weather and the availability of resources (natural environment) and religious dictates (cultural environment). It will also vary depending on the people who surround us (social environment), the degree of our genetic overlap with them, and such additional factors as their age and health, which bear on their capacity to reproduce and nurture. Let us narrow our focus still further and model a particular aid-giving dilemma. Assume that the social environment of A (aid-giver) is composed of just two people—A's child and A's mother. Both need aid today, but A can aid only one. Which will it be?

Sociobiologists would note that A is related to both by one-half, but A's child has more reproductive and nurturing time remaining. However, if A's child should be chronically ill, and A's parent healthy, weight would be added to the parent's side in the evolutionary calculus. It becomes important, in this calculus, to determine whether A is male or female. If A is female, the balance may swing a bit toward the child; if male, toward the mother.[18] In part, this is because although males and females are in the same position regarding identification of their mothers, no ascribed male parent can be as certain a child is his as an ascribed female parent can be that it is hers.[19] The reason is quite simple: although sociobiologists suggest we are programmed to differentiate between relatives in our aid-giving activity, we apparently have no innate automatic mechanism by which to recognize biological relatives.[20] Something in our environment tells us: A female is told that a child is hers by the objective evidence of its emergence from her womb. The evidence a male receives that a child is his is always less certain than that.

Another factor entering into the calculations as to whether aid will go to A's child or A's mother is the status of bonds of reciprocity between the parties. A may owe one of the contenders a favor, but not the other.

It should be obvious, at this point, that it would be prohibitively difficult, though theoretically possible, randomly to pinpoint individuals in various parts of the world today and predict with any certainty whether they will aid their child before their parent. Their environments and cultures, the idiosyncratic characteristics of their relatives, and the peculiarities of their interactions with those relatives will vary too greatly.[21] But if all the people of the world are viewed together, sociobiologists feel comfortable in predicting whether the *typical* or *average* person living today would favor the child versus the mother in our example. This is because with expanded population samples, extremes of environment and culture are neutralized; they counterbalance each other. Likewise, idiosyncratic and personal characteristics and conditions of aid-givers and contenders for aid counterbalance. For example, for every unhealthy child in a large population sample there is an unhealthy parent; the aid-givers themselves will be half female and half male; for every parent who is owed a favor due to a reciprocal bond, there is a child who is similarly owed a favor. With such variables neutralized and thus washed out of the picture, one is left with *universal constants* upon which predictions as to typical behavior can be made with reasonable certainty. Thus, parents and children are *always* related by one-half, but one's child is *always* younger than one's parent. So in the typical case, one will aid one's child before one's mother because the child has more lifetime remaining in which to reproduce and nurture representatives of one's genetic package.[22]

Similar calculations as to typical aid-giving behavior can be done with other sets of contenders for aid. Let us retain the child and replace the parent with a nephew. One's child is normally of the same generation as one's nephew (and in large population samples, their amalgamated typical ages will be virtually identical); thus, the child should have no edge when it comes to life expectancy in the typical case. Nevertheless, the child wins because of the genetic relatedness measure (one-half vs. one-fourth). In the case of a nephew and an aunt, although they are both related by one-fourth, typically the nephew should win, because nephews are normally *two* generations younger than aunts.

This is a good place to end our introductory overview of sociobiology, because our discussion of typical behavior prediction feeds into the next chapter, which examines how lawmakers regularly attempt to predict typical behavior in large populations under their jurisdiction. For now, let us leave science and bridge over to the law.

NOTES

1. Richard D. Alexander, in remarks to Midwestern Evolution and Human Behavior Conference, Ann Arbor, Michigan, April 12, 1987.
2. For an advanced treatment of the subject, see Williams, *Adaptation and Natural Selection*.
3. See E. O. Wilson, *Biophilia*, 46: "Darwin was a great expansionist. He shocked the world by arguing convincingly that life is the creation of an autonomous process so simple that it can be understood with just a moment of reflection. . . . It can all be summarized in a couple of lines: new variations in the hereditary material arise continuously, some survive and reproduce better than others, and as a result organic evolution occurs. And even more briefly as follows: natural selection acting on mutations produces evolution."
4. See generally Dawkins, *The Extended Phenotype*.
5. To a population geneticist "[a]n individual is fit if its adaptations are such as to make it likely to contribute a more than average number of genes to future generations" (Williams, *Adaptation and Natural Selection*, 158).
6. Although evolutionary biologists think that natural selection operates, at least primarily, at the level of the genes or genetic material that an individual (and that individual's kin) contains, there is some room in current thinking for the operation of selection at the level of whole populations of individuals. See Williams, *Adaptation and Natural Selection*, 92–250; Williams, ed., *Group Selection*; Barash, *Sociobiology and Behavior*, 2d ed., 107–15, 125–28, 137–38; Brandon and Burian, eds., *Genes, Organisms, Populations: Controversies over the Units of Selection*.
7. See Williams, *Adaptation and Natural Selection*, 83: "Complex systems

of behavior, such as the more elaborate reproductive patterns, will usually be a blend of learned and instinctive elements. There are things
that have to be learned, such as the individual characteristics of a particular mate or the location of a nest site. All elements that can be
instinctive, however, will be instinctive. Instinct costs less than learned
behavior in the currency of genetic information."

8. See Trivers, *Social Evolution*, 90, 94.
9. See Gould, *Ever Since Darwin*, 260–67.
10. "Estimates of [gene] mutation rates range from about 10^4 to 10^{10} per
generation" (Williams, *Adaptation and Natural Selection*, 24). See also
Trivers, *Social Evolution*, 91.
11. E.g., Trivers, *Social Evolution*, 262–63.
12. Hamilton, "The Evolution of Altruistic Behavior," 354; Hamilton, "The
Genetical Evolution of Social Behavior," 1, 16.
   Hamilton's exposition of kin selection is a cornerstone of sociobiology.
His rule states that selection will favor an action by one animal that
causes a loss to itself of c offspring, and a gain of b offspring to another
animal to which it is related by r, provided $rb - c > o$. For a nonmath-
ematical discussion of some of the intricate implications of Hamilton's
rule, see Grafen, "A Geometric View of Relatedness," 28.
13. See, e.g., Trivers, *Social Evolution*, 169–79.
14. See generally Dawkins, *The Selfish Gene*, 97–100; Alexander, *Darwinism
and Human Affairs*, 44, 45, 130, and Breuer, *Sociobiology and the Human
Dimension*, 11–16.
15. See generally Trivers, "The Evolution of Reciprocal Altruism."
16. See Alexander, *The Biology of Moral Systems*, 82, 94, 97, regarding the
complexities of direct and indirect reciprocity.
17. For an overview of the variation in approaches of certain social and
natural scientists to the interaction of genetic programming and culture,
see Boyd and Richerson, *Culture and the Evolutionary Process*, 12–14.
See also Ball, "Memes as Replicators," 145, 157. Examples can be found
in Alexander, "Evolution and Culture," 50; Cavilli-Sforza and Feldman,
Cultural Transmission and Evolution; Dawkins, *The Selfish Gene*, 203;
Durham, "Toward a Coevolutionary Theory of Human Biology and
Culture," 39; and Lumsden and Wilson, *Promethean Fire*.
18. For other reasons why human females are posited, *typically* (not uni-
versally or absolutely) to be *somewhat* more solicitous of ascribed offspring than are males, including the factual premise that females invest
more of their reproductive potential in any particular offspring than do
males, see Daly and Wilson, *Sex, Evolution, and Behavior*, and Symons,
The Evolution of Human Sexuality. See also Beckstrom, *Sociobiology and
the Law*, 81–88.
19. See Gaulin and Schlegel, "Paternal Confidence and Paternal Investment:
A Cross-Cultural Test of a Sociobiological Hypothesis"; Russell and
Wells, "Estimating Paternity Confidence"; and Kurland, "Paternity,
Mother's Brother, and Human Sociality."

Cf. the following statement by the Wyoming Supreme Court in an action to determine the paternity of a child: "The woman carries the child through pregnancy. When born of her, the fact of motherhood is obvious. Not so the man. The proof of fatherhood, or the proof of the lack thereof, must come from an external source." *A v. X, Y, and Z*, 641 P.2d 1222, 1225. (Wyo. 1982). Recent developments in embryo transplants would call for a slight modification of the Wyoming court's statement. The possibility of mix-ups in community maternity wards can also affect maternity confidence to some degree.

20. Barash, *The Whisperings Within*, 106, and Irons, "Kinship," 80-81. "[I]t has recently been shown that some insects have a specific chemical signal enabling them to recognize their kin by smell. It is not beyond the realm of possibility that a simple signal exists in humans as well—although I would be inclined to expect a visual rather than an olfactory signal" (Konner, *The Tangled Wing*, 321–22). See also Daly and Wilson, *Sex, Evolution, and Behavior*, 53. Cf. Alexander, *The Biology of Moral Systems*, 100: "[T]here is yet no undisputed evidence for unlearned recognition of relatives in any species."

21. See Irons, "Investment and Primary Social Dyads," for a discussion of how basic genetic programming that furthers the reproduction of genetic materials contained in we humans and our close genetic relatives ("inclusive fitness") may produce varying treatment of others depending on differences in environment. See also Kurland, "Paternity," 164-66, for a discussion of various idiosyncratic characteristics that can influence whether one invests in sons and daughters or nieces and nephews.

22. See Fisher, *The Genetical Theory of Natural Selection*, 27-30, on the possibility of quantifying the reproductive and nurturing value of a generation age difference.

Chapter

II

The Law and Averages

In the past when I have suggested to scientists that sociobiology might be used in the legal process, they have usually assumed I meant "goal-establishment normative uses" — uses implementing the idea that if evolution has given humans predispositions or tendencies toward certain types of behavior, then the law should aim to promote that behavior because it is "natural." There are deep philosophical problems with that idea — with moving from reportorial observations of behavioral tendencies to suggestions that they should be endorsed by society. Most thinkers, including sociobiologists, shy away from such uses of natural history. Chapter III will deal with this problem in more detail; so for now, let us assume that sociobiology can have little or no goal-establishment normative use in lawmaking. Nevertheless, it does have considerable impressive potential for contributing to the legal process.

We are just beginning to uncover ways in which sociobiological knowledge might aid the legal process, though several people have already written in the field.[1] My personal probing until recently has been guided by the assumption that lawmakers were measuring out impartial justice and could use assistance from behavioral science in their efforts. I have now focused on the fact that lawmakers are only human and are behaving as individuals when they function in their official capacities. Thus insights from evolutionary biology concerning human behavior may be useful in helping to ensure that impartial justice is achieved. I treat this subject in chapter VI.

Mostly, though, I have assumed, as my working basis, that lawmakers are operating impartially in a democratic framework, and I have looked for ways that sociobiology could help them achieve goals they have decided upon as being appropriate for their society—how the science could be *facilitative*. For example, I, and others, have detailed how sociobiology could help in the effort to regulate criminal activity of various sorts when deterrence is the goal,[2] how it could help to decide child custody disputes when the law attempts to serve the best interest of the children,[3] and how it could assist in efforts to reform marriage prohibition laws.[4] From these and many other examples, a common pattern emerges: legal authorities have made an assessment of average or typical behavior of some part of a population an important part of the solution of a legal problem.

Scientists unfamiliar with the legal process have often been puzzled when I have said that sociobiologists and lawmakers have a mutual interest in typical behavior. They may understand that an important focus of sociobiology is assessment of average or typical behavior in a population given various environmental circumstances, but when I say that an assessment of typical behavior is often instrumental in lawmaking, I am met by disbelief. I think this is due to the layperson's impression—or hope—that justice is individualized. I suppose we all would like to hear that when a legal decision involving us is made, it is based upon our *personal* actions, intentions, or whatever is relevant, and not on the attributes of someone else—even a hypothesized average or typical member of the population.

The law strives for individualized justice—laypeople can be reasonably assured of that. But the search for information on such things as a particular individual's behavior and intentions in order to provide individualized justice is frequently thwarted by practical limitations. In such circumstances lawmakers, of necessity, turn to an assessment of typical behavior of the population in the relevant locality. I can illustrate this with a subject that I have treated in detail elsewhere—intestate succession.[5] In this area legislatures have had to deal with the question of what to do with the property of people who die without a will (intestate). In respect to any particular deceased person, the authorities would like to know what the deceased intended—or would have intended—in that regard. Of course, the deceased is not available to testify, and any other evidence on the question (short of a duly executed will, which does not exist in this case, of course) is generally unacceptable. Lawmakers have solved this dilemma by creating schemes of distribution that purport to reflect what the *typical* decedent who did not write a will would have done with his[6] property if he had.

· Dilemmas like this have peppered the law with now-institutionalized instances of lawmakers attempting to detect or predict typical behavior patterns in a population in order to help solve legal problems.

Let me use, as another example, an area of the law that I will treat more fully later in this book.[7] There is a substantial body of cases in United States law reports, under the heading of contracts, in which litigants have approached the courts seeking compensation for services provided to another. It is agreed that the service was provided, but that there was no explicit contract for the service; the parties more or less drifted into the arrangement. Nevertheless, the courts in these cases apply the general rule of thumb used in contract disputes—they seek to carry out what the parties intended at the time they entered into the arrangement.

Typically in these cases, as evidence of the parties' earlier intentions, the party who provided the service says he expected to be compensated. The recipient of the service says he did not expect to have to pay for it. Both parties appear to be telling the truth. What is the court to do? If the court washes its hands of the matter and turns the parties away, it will, in effect, be deciding the case against the party asking for compensation. The courts have solved the dilemma by applying a tiebreaker derived from what they presume to be the *typical* expectations of parties under these circumstances.

The law of evidence can provide us with a third example of how typical behavior is important in lawmaking. When weighing the evidence that a witness gives on the stand on behalf of a party to litigation, U.S. legal authorities have decided that it is important to consider the relationship of the witness to the party in whose favor the testimony is given. As the veracity of a witness is usually difficult, if not impossible, to determine from the witness's words and demeanor, authorities have, as a corrective device, resorted to assumptions that people who bear various close relationships to one another are more inclined to stretch or forget the truth, etc., for each other's benefit than if they were comparative strangers to one another, and it is permissible to point out this probable bias during the course of a trial.[8] Those assumptions of testimonial bias are based on the lawmakers' impressions of typical or average behavior.

The illustrations I have given of how typical behavior is important in legal processes are just some of the many that have occurred to me from my limited vantage point.[9] With the concerted effort of experts in all the various areas of the law, I suspect that upwards to a hundred, maybe more, similar examples could be located.

Lawmakers, in their attempts to describe typical behavior when it is important to their tasks, have historically relied almost entirely on their own observations, reflective intuition, or plain gut feelings. Thoughtful lawmakers most certainly would have been willing to admit that frequently they could have been off the mark. But they did not have the luxury that pure scientists have of not reporting their impressions or theories for practical consumption until hard confirming evidence is available. Lawmakers have been forced to do the best they could under their own lights because they are called upon to make timely decisions. Most lawmakers would welcome any creditable help that is available.

In many, if not all, of the instances where typical behavior is or will be important to a legal task, social scientists with empirical research skills could doubtless provide lawmakers with comparatively hard evidence of actual typical behavior. But individualized empirical research on every type of legally significant typical behavior in relevant subsets of the population would require an ambitious, expensive, and time-consuming effort. It seems unlikely that such comprehensive assistance will be available to lawmakers. On the other hand, selective modest amounts of empirical research prompted by a knowledge of socio-biological theory is feasible. In what areas should it be done? How should priorities be determined? Here is where sociobiology can help lawmakers *today*.

It seems reasonable to assume that a major portion of surmises or predictions that lawmakers have made and will make about typical behavior patterns will agree with what sociobiologists predict. In those cases, if sociobiology is to have any immediate use for lawmakers, it might merely be to give them some comfort from an outside source that the observations or predictions they have arrived at independently are close to the mark. But in the areas where typical behavior is important to the law and impressionistic legal conclusions differ from sociobiological theory, the theory can serve a more active advisory role. Knowledge of the conflicting theory could prompt lawmakers to commission empirical studies of actual behavior to discover whether their impressions or the sociobiologists' predictions are closest to the facts of actual typical behavior.

This potential for immediate use of sociobiology by the legal system calls for illustrations. I will draw one from American tort law and a second from the law of the Netherlands regarding the disqualification of witnesses in lawsuits.

Empirical Behavioral Research Following Sociobiological Leads

United States Law: Torts

This subject is one that I have related to sociobiology in more detail elsewhere.[10] In recent years courts have been struggling with the question of whether to permit bystanders who observe an accident, such as an automobile striking a pedestrian, to recover compensation for alleged emotional damages the bystanders suffered as a result of their observation.[11] Some courts have been reluctant to extend the liability of the party accountable for the accident (the tortfeasor) in this way because of the difficulties of disproving alleged emotional or psychological damage to the bystander. When monetary recovery for such damages has been permitted, it generally has been limited to relatives of the victim of the physical impact. In an attempt to put some bounds on a tortfeasor's liabilities in this regard and help ensure the genuineness of claims, the Iowa Supreme Court recently circumscribed the relatives permitted to recover for such damages in its jurisdiction.[12] The line drawn by the court represented a judgment that the relatives permitted to recover were more likely, typically, to suffer emotional damages from observing the impact than those who were not permitted to recover; mothers, fathers, sons, daughters, siblings, and other close relatives were permitted to recover, but cousins, for example, were not. Sociobiologists will feel reasonably comfortable with such gross categorizations in large population samples — such as all people who will appear as bystander litigants in Iowa courts in the next several decades. Here is why.

Common experience, as well as documented research, teaches us that we can be subject to severe neurological and physiological repercussions from being personally endangered.[13] The lingering effects[14] may have an evolutionary adaptive function of impressing on us the need for taking avoidance action when faced with similar dangers in the future. Furthermore, we have noted the sociobiological position that we are programmed to be particularly concerned not only for our own welfare and survival, but also for that of others who bear a close genetic relationship to us. It should follow that the typical mother, for instance, who observes her child being endangered would react in much the same manner as if she herself were endangered. The reaction should be similar in character but probably not as severe, inasmuch as the child does not carry all of the mother's genes. The other family members who are also related to the impact victim by one-half — the father and siblings — may be typically expected to react not much differently from the mother. At least they all could be expected to have a more severe emotional reaction than the typical cousin of an impact victim, who is related by one-eighth. Thus the Iowa scheme that permits recovery by those related by one-half to the impact victim but not by cousins and others related by one-eighth or less seems sociobiologically sound if lines must be drawn.

However, there is one aspect of the Iowa scheme that should raise sociobiologists' eyebrows. Bystanders may recover when their grandparents are impact victims, but not when their uncles, aunts, nieces, or nephews are the victims.[15] From the evolutionary biologist's viewpoint this categorization is highly suspect—all of the named relatives are related to the bystanders by one-fourth. However, aunts/uncles and nephews/nieces are, on the average, one and three generations younger, respectively, than grandparents. The younger people, therefore, have more remaining reproductive and nurturing potential. On that basis sociobiologists would expect that the typical bystander would be more solicitous toward the niece/nephew or aunt/uncle than toward the grandparent and would have corresponding emotional reactions when observing them endangered. Therefore, if bystanders are permitted to recover when their grandparents are the impact victims, sociobiologists would suspect that recovery should also be permitted when their uncles and aunts and, yet more clearly, their nieces and nephews, are the impact victims (primarily focusing on relatedness and reproductive value).

Of course, other operative factors, such as local environment and culture or generalized reciprocal altruism patterns may alter the basic picture just outlined and justify this aspect of the Iowa scheme. But sociobiological theory generates a suspicion that the Iowa court was wrong in this particular, in view of its announced purposes for line drawing. The suspicion is sufficient to warrant a study by empirical researchers. They could, for example, administer a questionnaire giving grandmother, aunt, and niece as paired alternatives and ask interviewees which one they would rescue if they could rescue only one.[16] The answers from a representative sample of the population in Iowa ought to be of interest to lawmakers there. And similar studies prompted by a knowledge of sociobiological theory could provide useful information to lawmakers in other states who are contemplating the question of circumscribing bystander/relatives permitted to recover for emotional distress.

Netherlands Law: Evidence

All of my attempts to relate sociobiology to the solution of legal problems have thus far been focused on U.S. legal systems or, at least, those systems with origins in English common law. This merely reflects my personal limitations. Surely whatever sociobiology has to offer legal systems has applicability outside the Anglo-American sphere. As an illustration of that, let us venture onto the European continent and into the Roman-influenced civil law sphere for our second example of how sociobiological theory might prompt empirical research that could assist in the solution of legal problems.

The statutory laws of the Netherlands contain a provision that generally disqualifies people from testifying in certain lawsuits when they are lineal relatives of a party to the action (a party's parents, grandparents, etc., or children, grandchildren, etc.).[17] This disqualification does not apply to other genetic relatives of the parties.[18] Commentators have suggested that there are two aspects to the disqualification: On the one hand, if the relative's testimony were to disfavor the party, it might create disharmony in the family—an occurrence that lawmakers were anxious to avoid, even at the cost of forgoing pertinent evidence.[19] On the other hand (and most important for our purposes), if the relative's testimony were to favor the party, it would be unreliable because of the closeness of the relationship.[20] In other words, the lawmakers were fearful that the disqualified relatives would shade the truth, tell half-truths, and the like, to favor the party. Presumably this judgment by the lawmakers was based upon an impression of typical conduct among close relatives.

Notice again that collateral (nonlineal) relatives of a party, such as siblings, aunts/uncles, and nephews/nieces, are not disqualified by the Netherlands' provision. In our previous review of sociobiological hypotheses we have seen reasons why scientists might think that the Netherlands' categorizations of those relatives disqualified and those qualified to testify may not be artfully drawn, given the goal of excluding unreliable testimony.

Presumably the patterns of aid-giving that sociobiologists would predict in large population samples, such as all people appearing in the Netherlands' courts, would translate into testimonial manipulation of facts in order to favor close relatives. If that is true, then the Netherlands' related witness disqualification list may be either underinclusive or overinclusive. If a person's grandson, for example, cannot testify in the person's behalf, then that person's sister probably should not be permitted to so testify either—or both should be permitted to testify—inasmuch as, typically, everything else being equal, a sister (one-half related) would be predicted to aid her sibling to the same or a greater degree as a grandson (one-fourth related) would be predicted to aid his grandparent.

Again, however, local environment and culture, including generalized reciprocal relation patterns, may be acting in such a way as to justify the Netherlands' categorizations. But there is enough of a discrepancy indicated here between what lawmakers in the Netherlands seem to have presumed about typical behavior of people appearing in their courts and what sociobiologists would predict about that behavior to justify an empirical study of what that behavior really is. It is not as easy to visualize a research design here as it was in the previous example regarding emotional disturbance resulting from observing a tortious impact to a relative. I suspect, however, that empiricists could devise ways to measure willingness to shade the truth in behalf of various relatives without violating ground rules governing experimentation with human subjects. If not, then this legal problem area could be a candidate for long-range assistance from sociobiology of the sort I will discuss shortly.

Simultaneous Testing of Behavioral Hypothesis

First we should note something at this point that has probably already occurred to many readers who are scientists. Empirical research following sociobiological leads could not only give lawmakers useful information concerning typical behavior important for their purposes, but the *same research*, if properly tailored, could also serve as tests of the behavioral hypotheses that prompt the research: two birds could be killed with one stone. And, not incidentially, funding could be sought from two directions—law- and science-oriented sources. Thus a fertile ground would appear to exist here for mutually beneficial cooperative research between scientists and lawyers.[21]

Direct Use of Sociobiology by Lawmakers in Assessing Typical Behavior

It is important to observe that the potential we have just explored—for immediate use of sociobiology to prompt empirical research on actual typical behavior important to the law—does not entail the direct use of sociobiological theory to inform lawmakers on such matters. The theory would only be used as a signal, in a given case, that a study of actual behavior should be commissioned. However, I do not mean to suggest by this that sociobiology, when and if it becomes well settled and substantiated, should not be directly employed by lawmakers searching for typical behavior.

Differences in detail now exist among sociobiologists in their hypotheses concerning typical behavior. With time, consensus is likely to develop on an ever-increasing number of concepts. Again, with time, those concepts may be confirmed by ongoing empirical testing. Eventually an intricate theoretical web concerning human behavior, woven from genetic, mathematical, and evolutionary biological threads, may be made concrete by empirical testing in fields like anthropology and psychology.

When sociobiological theory is thus firmed up, responsible authorities should study the structure and decide whether some aspects of the total pattern could be used as an additive or corrective to lawmakers' impressions of typical behavior. Such an application might be particularly useful in areas like the intestate succession laws, where lawmakers are attempting to reflect what sort of property disposition the typical person dying without a will would have made if he or she had written one. That behavioral question is imagined—it never happens, so it cannot be observed. Thus it would be fruitless for lawmakers to employ empirical researchers to discover actual behavior in this case when the impressions of lawmakers and sociobiological theory differ regarding the people to whom typical intestate decedents would have disposed their property. If sociobiology were to assist the law here, it would have to be used in a direct manner on the assumption that sociobiological predictions as to typical aid-giving behavior are a better representation of what dead people would have done than any other information lawmakers could gather.[22]

I would expect initial resistance to such direct use of substantiated sociobiology to come from members of the legal profession who have had experience in dealing with witnesses expert in what one might call "soft" science. Lawyers have found, for example, that expert opinions as to when someone should be considered insane and thus legally irresponsible have been based on shifting sands.[23] From this and similar experiences, judges, in particular, have become wary of the social sciences, often preferring to rely on their own impressions or those of lay jurors. For good reason, they have generally been more receptive to information from "hard" sciences like mathematics and physics. Sociobiology is social science in that it addresses human interactive behavior; however, its foundations are in genetics, mathematics, and the economic logic of natural processes. Its way of looking at the world is congenial to those trained, as lawyers are, in logical analysis. The few lawyers I know who have taken the time to look deeply into evolutionary biology have all been favorably impressed. I suspect that as growing numbers of lawyers learn sociobiology, the problem will not be to convince them to use it in their profession, but rather to wait until it has been well tested. There is no need to wait, however, to engage in empirical research on *actual* behavior when sociobiological theory differs from what lawmakers have presumed to be typical behavior. That can be done immediately.

NOTES

1. See, e.g., Hirschleifer, "Privacy: Its Origin, Function, and Future"; Epstein, "A Taste for Privacy? Evolution and the Emergence of a Naturalistic Ethic"; Beckstrom, "Sociobiology and Intestate Wealth Transfers"; Rodgers, "Bringing People Back: Toward a Comprehensive Theory of Taking in Natural Resources Law"; Schwartz, "On the Prospects of Using Sociobiology in Shaping Laws: A Cautionary Note"; and Alexander, *The Biology of Moral Systems*, 180–86. See also limited discussions in Rawls, *A Theory of Justice*, 502–4, and Posner, *The Economics of Justice*, 186–87. See generally Beckstrom, *Sociobiology and the Law*, and Elliott, "The Evolutionary Tradition in Jurisprudence."

2. See Beckstrom, *Sociobiology and the Law*, 127–34, regarding stepparent child abuse. See also Alexander, *The Biology of Moral Systems*, 220–21 (rape); Thornhill and Thornhill, "Human Rape: An Evolutionary Analysis," and Daly and Wilson, *Homicide*.

3. Beckstrom, *Sociobiology and the Law*, 75–92, 134–36, and "Die Elterliche Fürsorge als Entscheidungskriterium in Sorgerechtsverfahren" (Practical Legal Applications of Sociobiology: The Solicitude Factor in Interparental Child Custody Disputes).

4. Beckstrom, *Sociobiology and the Law*, 117–23.

5. Ibid., 7–59, and Beckstrom, "Sociobiology and Intestate Wealth Transfers."

6. There is some justification for not using the more cumbersome her/his in the text here because there has been a slight tendency for the typical decedent who dies without a will in the U.S. to be male rather than female (Beckstrom, *Sociobiology and the Law*, 19).

7. See infra, chapter VII.

8. See Wigmore, 3A *Evidence* §949. In "Behavioral Research on Aid-Giving that Can Assist Lawmakers while Testing Scientific Theory," 33–35, I explored the message that sociobiology might hold for the law in regard to handling the testimony of one identical twin that is offered in behalf of the other.

9. People who are juror candidates can be "challenged for cause" and thus disqualified in U.S. courts when they are shown to be related within specified degrees of consanguinity or affinity to parties in the lawsuit. See 47 *Am. Jur. 2d*, "Jury," §313 (1969 and Supp. 1986); 50 *C.J.S.*, "Juries," §218 (1947 and Supp. 1986). See also Beckstrom, *Sociobiology and the Law*, at 136, regarding interpretation of words used in wills, and at page 99, regarding circumscribing who can recover emotional damages from observing a tortious injury to a relative.

10. Beckstrom, *Sociobiology and the Law*, 99–113.

11. E.g., *Barnhill v. Davis*, 300 N.W. 2d 104 (Iowa 1981).

12. See generally Leibson, "Recovery of Damages for Emotional Distress Caused by Physical Injury to Another," and Simons, "Psychic Injury

and the Bystander: The Transcontinental Dispute between California and New York."

13. Bourne, "Military Psychiatry and the Vietnam Experience," 481, 486; Buck, Parke, and Buck, "Skin Conductance, Heart Rate, and Attention to the Environment in Two Stressful Situations," 95.

14. S. Cohen, "Aftereffects of Stress on Human Performance and Social Behavior: A Review of Research and Theory."

15. See Beckstrom, *Sociobiology and the Law*, 107–12.

16. Freedman, *Human Sociobiology*, 115, refers to an empirical study by H. Ginsburg in which grandparents were asked to choose between saving children or grandchildren. The children prevailed except when they were beyond the reproductive years; then there was a tendency to "save" the potentially reproductive grandchildren. The Ginsburg study appears never to have been published, but it was reported in a paper read to the Psychonomic Society in Washington, D.C., November, 1977 (ibid., 217). The apparent results of the Ginsburg study would comport with sociobiological theory. See Fisher, *The Genetical Theory of Natural Selection*, 27–30.

17. See Burgerlijk Wetboek, Vijfde Boek, Derde Titel, Art. 1947, in Fruin, ed., *De Nederlandse Wetboeken*, 589. A bill to revise Art. 1947 has been pending. See Pitlo, *Het Nederlandse Burgerlijk Wetboeken*, Deel 4, Bewijs en Verjaring, 169. I wish to acknowledge translation assistance by Martine De Proost-Ford and Phillip Hinnekens.

   Other European countries have had similar provisions, which appear to have origins in the Napoleonic Code and perhaps Roman law. Essentially the same provision in Italy was held unconstitutional as against the general right to be heard. Certoma, *The Italian Legal System*, 205.

18. Spouses and lineal in-laws are also disqualified (Burgerlijk Wetboek, Vijfde Boek, Derde Titel, Art. 1947, in Fruin, ed., *De Nederlandse Wetboeken*, 589).

19. Asser, *Handleiding Tot De Beoefening Van Het Nederlands Burgerlijk Recht*, Vijfde Deel-van Bewijs, 238–44.

20. Ibid. and Pitlo, *Het Nederlandse Burgerlijk Wetboecken*, 90.

21. See generally Beckstrom, "Behavioral Research on Aid-Giving."

22. Empirical studies have been done on actual wills in an effort to discover distributive patterns. See, e.g., Smith, Kish, and Crawford, "Inheritance of Wealth as Human Kin Investment"; Dunham, "The Method, Process and Frequency of Wealth Transmission at Death"; Ward and Beuscher, "The Inheritance Process in Wisconsin"; and Sussman, Cates, and Smith, *The Family and Inheritance*. There are, however, various reasons why the distributive patterns in wills will not reflect accurately what the typical person who dies in the future (for which intestate succession laws are perforce enacted) without a will would want done with his or her property. See Beckstrom, *Sociobiology and the Law*, 8–11.

23. See Schwartz, "On the Prospects of Using Sociobiology in Shaping Laws," 17-18.

III

Limits on Using Sociobiology: Normative Use

Up to now, in this book and earlier writings, I have discussed the potential for the use of sociobiological learning in various situations in the legal process.[1] In each of those situations the scientific learning would not be introduced to the process until *after* authorities had decided upon a goal that they hoped could be achieved through legal measures. The science would facilitate achievement of the goals. For example, from whatever inspirational sources, lawmakers have decided to distribute the property of a person who dies without a will in the way that the typical person who dies like that would want the property distributed,[2] and lawmakers have decided that in child custody disputes it is important to try to determine which of the contending adults can be predicted to be most solicitous of the child's welfare.[3] Sociobiology clearly has considerable potential for facilitating the achievement of such goals.

Now I want to look at the issue of goal establishment. I will examine the question whether the human natural history that evolutionary biology may reveal is a potential source of standards that lawmakers, as social planners, might use to *establish* goals to be promoted through the legal process.

Goals emerge, in the American legal system, from the process called policy-making. Policy-making and consequent goal establishment can occur in respect to any area of human concern from the mundane to the cosmic — from the disposal of city garbage to the exploration of outer space. Conscious or unconscious policy-making occurred, for example, as a preliminary to American lawmakers deciding upon the goal of distributing the property of people who die without a will in the way the typical person who so dies would want it distributed. Can human natural history provide a basis from which to initially arrive at such goals or to assess the rectitude of those that are already established? That is the main focus of this chapter, although I will return to the potential goal facilitation function of sociobiology toward the end.

I will be drawing from a body of literature bearing on the question of whether the sociobiological account of human natural history is a source for guidance regarding societal goals. Social planners, including lawmakers, should be interested in a scientific source that might tell them what is *desirable*, as well as what is *possible*, in human social engineering. Their interest in what is possible is rather obvious: quite simply, they do not want to embark on programs that will fail. That is a waste of resources (and bad for their image). The reasons why they should be interested in a scientific source of desirable social goals may be less obvious, particularly if the social planners are lawmakers in a representative political system. One may argue that the function of the lawmakers is simply to reflect what their constituencies want. Unfortunately, no sizable constituency exists that gives off clear, consistent messages as to what it wants. Thus, even if social planners should look to their constituencies exclusively for program goals, they are likely to find outside sources useful as clarifying or catalyzing devices for dealing with conflicting or undecipherable messages they receive from their constituencies.[4]

Furthermore, lawmakers in a representative system, together with social planners belonging more to the private sector, may assume a leadership role and attempt to determine, in the abstract, what goals are desirable for their society. When social planners assume such a detached posture, the value to them of any source of guidance, such as religious or secular dogma—and science, is fairly obvious.[5]

Thus I believe we can conclude that lawmakers should be interested in whatever the literature holds regarding the sociobiological account of human natural history as a source for determining limits on social planning and desirable goals for such plans. I will deal with these practical questions. Let me say here that what I report will be disappointing to those seeking social planning goals, but encouraging to those who want to believe that *any* goal might possibly be achieved.

Before dealing with the practical, direct questions of social planning goals and limitations, we need to review the literature regarding a matter that constitutes important background. There is much discussion in sociobiological writings about natural constraints on behavior versus free will to determine that behavior. Virtually all such discussion is in an abstract, or at best, an individual-person orientation. It is clear that sociobiologists consider the issue of free will to be important for social (group) engineering questions.[6] And lay intuition tells one that it must be. However, the mechanics of how behavioral constraints and free will from a single-person orientation translate into what might be accomplished by social (group) engineering have not been well developed. It is safe to assume there is a connection. Certainly some will, free or otherwise, must be exercised by social planners themselves to enact a social program, and, presumably, the will of the population upon which the program operates is crucial to its successful operation. So, before moving to what the literature says regarding goals for, and limits on, social planning, we should review what has been said about constraints on behavior and free will.

Genetic Constraints on Behavior versus Free Will

When sociobiology first came into public notice in the mid-1970s, one of the many brushfires it ignited involved the question of whether, and the extent to which, evolutionary biology allowed for present-day humans to exercise free will. A central proposition is now clear in sociobiological texts: natural history has brought humans to a point where each individual is programmed to be *predisposed* toward behavior that favors reproduction of the genetic complement the individual contains. That general, unqualified proposition is alarming to many who are committed, for one reason or another, to the idea that human behavior is flexible, allowing us to do just about whatever we wish if we put mind and will to it. Sociobiology has been labeled genetic "determinism" by some.[7] That labeling, at best, represents a misunderstanding. Properly interpreted, *a predisposition* to behave in a certain manner does not mean one is locked into a specific type of behavior in a given circumstance — that the outcome has been determined for us before the game even begins.

But I do not mean to suggest that the misunderstanding can be reduced to a clear question of semantics. The general sociobiological proposition was not succinctly stated and developed in one place in the early sociobiological writing that received most popular attention.[8] And many antideterminists have been too alarmed to be generous and circumspect in their interpretation of what they pick out of sociobiological texts. They read into what they know of human sociobiology a worst-case scenario from their standpoint. They suppose it means we are quite "hard-wired," both in our behavior and in the mental processes leading to it, so that we operate much like less complicated living organisms. Culture and learning, let alone ethics, have no place in such a supposed scheme.

Within four years after the public's initial introduction to sociobiology, several writers had come out with more detailed explanations of the contribution that evolutionary biology can make to human behavior studies.[9] At this point, the discipline perhaps should have been renamed something like "human biocultural science," but the name human sociobiology has persisted. There should be no harm in that as long as one keeps the following in mind: all acknowledged sociobiologists agree that environment and its cultural component are important—possibly more important than genetic predispositions—in determining the totality of human behavior.

Although sociobiologists differ in certain theoretical details, there is general agreement on the following outline: When human evolution reached the point where things identifiable as culture arrived on the scene, a coevolutionary process began. Natural selection continued to confer an advantage on any comparatively "hard-wired" and inflexible genetic programming that worked well in the environments in which humans moved. But now those whose mental and neural mechanisms were, through mutations and other difference-producing genetic processes, better able to learn from their environments and apply that learning, also gained a survival and reproductive advantage. And the "environment" had now broadened to contain culture—such as the information gained firsthand (from trial and error) or secondarily (from information gained through others) that sticks, stones, and fire could be used advantageously.

As human society and its cultural artifacts, devices, and ideas became more complex, a survival and reproductive premium went to those whose genetic programming allowed for flexibility in learning, planning with, and employing culture in the many and various environments—from lifetime to lifetime and from minute to minute—in which humans might find themselves. Natural selection was working on another dimension.

When a trait appears in the gene pool that confers a selective advantage in survival and reproduction, many generations must pass before it can become generally prevalent in the pool. There is always a multigenerational lag time. There is some disagreement as to the minimum amount of time it takes for a genetically influenced bit of behavior, such as a given degree of flexibility in response to the environment, to become generally prevalent in the human gene pool through the processes of natural selection.[10] However, it seems quite certain that natural selection has resulted in all humans now alive containing genetic programming for flexible response to the environment that was optimum for living conditions several thousand years ago, if not today.[11]

Our knowledge of living conditions, say ten thousand years ago, is not extensive, but it seems fairly clear that our ancestors were then group-living social animals.[12] Group living conferred advantages on the individual participants, or else it was unlikely that it would have existed. But here we must return to a basic sociobiological tenet: each person within the group carried a particularized genetic package, and was programmed to pursue his or her own genetic survival and reproductive agenda. This had to create a behavioral tension. To gain the advantages of group living while pursuing one's own agenda called for compromises. One's wants or needs regularly had to be diluted, achieved in indirect ways, or postponed. The evolved capacity for thoughtful flexibility allowed for such compromises.

But how flexible have human beings become? More to the point of our focus, how "ethical" can they be in their dealings with others? Can they not only take half-portions and postpone their own genetic interests in deference to that of others, but act frequently, or at least on occasion, in an extremely "ethical" manner by aiding others when there is virtually no likelihood of an eventual return to themselves or other individuals who contain high percentages of their genetic material? Sociobiologists have hesitated to answer such questions and for good reason. The issue is sensitive and momentous, and the evidence bearing upon it is complex and not yet clear. Let us look at what some of the leading sociobiologists have said on the subject.

Richard Alexander, Charles Lumsden, and Edward O. Wilson have made essentially the same observation here. After explaining flexible programming, they emphasize that any disposition one has to act on an occasion in a given manner is the result of interaction between (1) genetic programming to act flexibly, but toward generalized goals (the survival and reproduction of their genes most generally), *and* (2) the particular environment individuals find themselves in at any moment.[13] And the "environment" of individuals includes what is going on in their heads as well as what is going on outside of them![14] Thus to the extent that individuals know and appreciate human natural history, it will facilitate their breaking out of channelized modes of conduct. In other words, whatever free will we have without a knowledge of our natural history, it should be freer yet when we gain that knowledge and use it.[15] For example, if we fully realize we are programmed to enjoy and be driven toward copulation solely to reproduce our genes, we may gain the incentive and willpower to thwart that process (on occasion, if not permanently), liberate ourselves, and use the time saved to benefit our independent existence by reading, listening to music, or doing other things to broaden our experiences.[16]

Lumsden and Wilson go on to observe that our ethical precepts are based upon our behavioral predispositions and that those precepts, therefore, can be similarly altered by the exercise of free will or freer will gained through knowledge of our natural history.[17] For example, when we realize that we have a programmed inclination to render aid first and foremost to close genetic relatives, we may gain incentive and willpower to channel more aid to comparative strangers. Alexander has suggested that this could occur generally in the population if for no other reason than that aid-givers would thus *appear* more altruistic in contradiction to the revelation regarding our aid-giving predispositions. That would make them better candidates, in the eyes of their unrelated associates, for additional reciprocal relations that could eventually redound to the benefit of their genetic material.[18]

But are we still constrained so that however complex and convoluted our conscious or unconscious calculations may be, we will only act beneficently when we are expecting some eventual return to our genetic complement from whatever concessions we make to others? Richard Dawkins "hopes" not. He allows that we may be capable of "truly" altruistic behavior,[19] and he makes an empirical observation we can all make: we *at least* have the power to substitute our long-term genetic interests for those of the short term.[20] We can, for example, forgo the use of money and natural resources today in the hope or expectation that our descendants will benefit from them in the future.

Alexander has also noted that we, as individuals, can be manipulated in our efforts to serve our genetic reproductive interests. Each of us has enough flexibility in our programming to respond in "altruistic" ways to the collective pressure of the group in which we are embedded when our long-term interests are best served by remaining in good standing with the group. Lawmaking becomes relevant here: we can be made to *give* when a failure to do so is likely to cause others in our social fabric to impose costs greater than the expense of the beneficence.[21] Paying income taxes and stopping at traffic lights are obvious illustrations of this.

With that review of the sociobiological view of free will and the confidence that it is relevant to group or social planning, let me move to more direct, practical questions that social planners may have for sociobiologists.

Can Knowledge of Human Natural History Provide a Source of Goals for Social Planners?

There is a full body of literature now by critics of sociobiology, as well as sociobiologists themselves, to the effect that the discipline should not be used to establish societal norms and goals. The fear is that such use could result in the occurrence of ideologies such as social Darwinism, which many decades ago extended what was then known and hypothesized about natural history to justify laissez-faire, conservative positions.[22] Social Darwinism, it has been said, was behind the U.S. Supreme Court's overturn, as unconstitutional, in the early decades of this century, of legislation that had provided for minimum wages and restricted hours of work and child labor.[23] In today's context, the fear of many is that the picture drawn by evolutionary biology of humans having certain behavioral inclinations evolved through natural history will be used by ideologists to argue that the inclinations are "natural" and, therefore, right. An extension of that argument into the legal arena would call for the promotion, or at least tolerance, of the inclination. For example, if there is an inclination for humans to promote the interests of themselves and their close relatives, then laws that gave maximum free reign to self-interested pursuits would be indicated (is this "conservative"?). Another variation of such an argument could be that if humans have evolved to cooperate and engage in reciprocal altruism with comparative strangers in certain environmental circumstances, then laws should be enacted that promote such circumstances (is this "liberal"?).

Countless such arguments can be imagined if one picks and chooses from among the various facets of natural historical fact and theory. And there is something there for virtually everyone.[24] The possibilities are much the same as with seminal writings like the Bible, where one can find arguable support for many ethical positions, sometimes in conflict with one another.

There may be more hard, or scientific, fact and less theory in sociobiology than in the Bible, but that does not mean that any arguments drawn from sociobiology to support selected societal goals are any more right, pure, or true. Very simply, if we can agree that something did or does exist, we have not thereby established a desirable future standard or goal. *"Is" does not equal "ought."* This proposition may or may not seem obvious to the reader: in any case, it has been the focal point of volumes of philosophical discourse.[25] I believe the italicized phrase distills the present consensus of philosophers of science. Let me offer the most comprehensive illustration I can imagine that incorporates evolutionary biology.

If science tells us, as a fact, that humans have existed in essentially their present form for eons, it does not, *thereby*, follow that the human species *ought* to continue indefinitely and that we should take steps to achieve that end. Any such normative conclusion and goal must be derived from somewhere outside of the facts that natural science can tell us.

In addition to telling us of the facts of human existence, natural science may be able to tell us another type of interesting fact. It may be able to inform us of biologically based *facts* about *why* you and I think (if we do) that the human species ought to continue indefinitely[26]— not why it *should* continue indefinitely, but why you and I *think* it should. A third person might think that humankind should be eliminated when it seriously threatens to extinguish other life forms on earth. Science may be able to explain a factual, biological base for that thought also—but natural science cannot tell us which, if either, of these thoughts is "right" or "true."[27]

Similarly, bringing the point down to a narrower illustration, if science establishes that humans have had, for eons and to date, an inclination toward selfish behavior, that does not mean, ipso facto, that such behavior is desirable and should be encouraged.

Descriptions by evolutionary biologists of the natural history of *why* we act and think as we do or their descriptions of *how* we might manipulate natural processes to achieve social goals we have in mind have sometimes been interpreted as meaning the scientists are saying that natural history indicates that which we *ought* to do in the future. Interpretive debates along these lines have an unreal quality for me, as if we are discussing the question of whether natural science can point to a stone and thereby change the stone into a principle.

However, the responsibility for this interpretive problem has not resided completely with the readers of sociobiological writings. Some sociobiological writers have illustrated how human natural history might be used, informatively, to facilitate the achievement of societal goals, while leaving it unclear where they derived the goals they used in their illustrations. It has thus been possible to read them as suggesting that the goals were found somewhere in the science. Let me give you an example, from Edward O. Wilson's writings, that has drawn criticism from inside the evolutionist camp.[28] This example also illustrates the importance of distinguishing, and keeping in mind, the difference between aims or objectives in focus (let us call them goals), on one hand, and social or environmental conditions that can help us achieve the goals, on the other hand. If natural science is of no help to us in deciding what our goals ought to be, it may at least indicate social or environmental conditions that would best be created or maintained if the goals we select, regardless of that science, are to be achieved.[29]

The example is from *On Human Nature*, where Wilson develops a thought in a long paragraph. He begins by saying, "I believe that a correct application of evolutionary theory . . . favors diversity in the gene pool as a cardinal value."[30] Taken out of context, this could be interpreted as a statement that diversity in the gene pool is a goal to be derived from natural science. But a careful further reading of the paragraph indicates Wilson is instead saying that maintenance of diversity in the gene pool is a way to *facilitate* the achievement of another goal he has in mind. He seems to be suggesting that *if* the current frequency of emergence in the population of humans of extraordinary physical and mental capacity is desirable, and we wish to continue *it* as a goal, *then* diversity in the gene pool should be maintained (and its maintenance should be a "cardinal value"). Diversity in the gene pool will facilitate achievement of the goal. Wilson goes on to cite work by George Williams on population genetics that supports his observation. He ends by observing that achievement of the goal could not alternatively be achieved by a contrived program of eugenics without "an unimaginably greater knowledge of human heredity" than we now have. But (and this is the important point) he does not say that the goal he has in focus in the paragraph—the maintenance of the present frequency of extraordinary individuals emerging—can be derived from natural science.[31] I am sure he would contend that if you or I (or he) should think such a goal desirable, the mechanics of our thinking will eventually be traceable in evolutionary biological terms. That is clear from his later writings,[32] as is his observation that natural science is not in a position, presently at least, to prove to lawmakers, or to the rest of us, that any such goal is desirable or correct in an objective sense.[33]

So, what is the message in the literature for those looking today to evolutionary biology for guidance in selecting goals for their social programs? I read it as this: A knowledge of human natural history cannot provide us with goals.[34] Natural science can, however, suggest norms, values, standards, or guides (pick your word) that one would be advised to follow if one wishes to *achieve* certain independently arrived at, predetermined goals.[35] In other words, *the promise that evolutionary biology holds for social planners rests in looking backward, once goals have been selected, to natural history for facilitative guides and not in working forward from natural history to establish the goals.*

Does Sociobiology Reveal Limits
on Human Social Engineering?

If evolutionary biology cannot tell social planners what ultimate goals *ought* to be pursued, can it reveal whether there are goals that cannot be achieved because of natural human behavioral limitations? On this question sociobiologists offer optimism to those social planners who would like to think they have a free hand. Without distinguishing between individual and group or societal efforts, Alexander has said he regards "humans as sufficiently plastic in their behavior to accomplish *almost* anything they wish" (emphasis mine)[36] and, further, that "[e]volutionary understanding . . . has the power to make humans sufficiently plastic to accomplish *whatever they wish*" (emphasis Alexander's).[37] Wilson writes as follows:

> Human nature is not just the array of outcomes attained in existing societies. It is also the potential array that might be achieved through conscious design by future societies. By looking over the realized social systems of hundreds of animal species and deriving the principles by which these systems have evolved, we can be certain that all human choices represent only a tiny subset of those theoretically possible.[38]

It seems that if social planners are looking for absolute limits on what can be accomplished, they will have to look elsewhere. However, as can be seen in the above quotations, Alexander and Wilson outline unlimited horizons on the assumption that some element of the population understands the history of evolution. Undoubtedly that would have to include the social planners themselves. It might also require an understanding by a large proportion of the general population of programs which had particularly innovative aspects, so that the population would accept and absorb the innovations.

Now, lazy social planners—or, to be more gentle, the ones who must act today and cannot wait for the time when the required proportion of the population understands evolutionary history—may ask what limitations exist in the absence of such an understanding. On this question the leading sociobiologists have been intentionally obscure. Alexander has probably treated this question more extensively than any other sociobiologist. In the last sentence of the following paragraph from his 1979 book, *Darwinism and Human Affairs*, he addresses the question; the rest of the paragraph contains his reasons for being obscure in that last sentence:

> As it concerns social behavior, human nature would seem to be represented by our learning capabilities and tendencies in different situations.

The limits of human nature, then, could be identified by discovering those things that we cannot learn. But there is a paradox in this, for to understand human nature would then be to know how to change it—how to create situations that would enable or cause learning that could not previously occur. To whatever extent that is so, the limits of human nature become will-o'-the-wisps that inevitably retreat ahead of our discoveries about them. Even if this is not true in all respects, I believe that it must be true in some of the most important and practical ones. I regard it as illusory to identify social behavior far outside present human capabilities (or interests) and then suggest that one has somehow said something significant about the limits of human nature, and similarly illusory to note any current human failure in social matters and regard it as unchangeable. In this light I suggest that there is much in this book that deals appropriately with human nature and its limits, though it may not always be readily identifiable as such to those who have formed opinions alternative to that expressed here.[39]

Alexander probably regretted adding the last sentence to the paragraph I quote above, for fear that, in spite of his prior qualifying remarks, people would use that last sentence in isolation as a reason for searching through his book to locate limits on human social behavior capacities. I say this because in 1987 he omitted the last sentence when otherwise quoting the paragraph verbatim and then said: "If there are any truly unalterable limits to human social learning (and I am not willing to admit that there are), then I would still contend that (1) they have not been identified, and to do so would be extremely difficult, and (2) they are of little significance to anyone."[40]

In sum, I take Alexander to be telling us that any present "limitations" on what social behavior humans can learn are unidentified and that any that exist are not *really* limitations, because they can probably all be altered or eliminated once we study and learn the natural mechanisms that have (for the moment) created the limitations.

I suspect that in his treatment of the question of present human social behavioral limitations, Alexander is being about as direct as any natural scientist can be, given (1) the virtually limitless, mind-boggling array of human social behavioral manifestations that exist and could be imagined and (2) the nascent condition of human behavioral science, including its sociobiological input. Furthermore, as Alexander suggests, if one were to attempt a mapping of present human behavioral limitations for practical consumption, any assigned limits would tend to be either dubious or obvious and would depend, in any case, on the time frame one has in mind. For example, first using socially indifferent behavior, let me *declare* that no human living today has the capability of running a mile in under three minutes, forty seconds (dubious),[41] or under three minutes flat (obvious). But in five years, or fifty years, can we learn enough about nutrition, body training, and, indeed, genetic engineering, to accomplish both of those times? Similarly, using social behavior, if humans cannot typically be expected today irretrievably to sacrifice their personal interests for those of only two siblings[42] or one stranger, can we learn enough about natural history and genetics to accomplish both of those ends given enough time? It appears that no sociobiologist, at least, would say we cannot.

So sociobiologists have little to offer on the issue of what social goals are unachievable because of human behavioral limitations — they suggest future horizons are unlimited in that respect. No goal is achieved without cost, however. Here is where sociobiological accounts of natural science can clearly make a contribution to social planning — by suggesting costs of any contemplated social programs that planners may want to weigh before embarking on the programs. Let us turn now to an illustration of how natural science might uncover such costs and otherwise provide sources of aid in the planning and execution of contemplated social programs.

The Potential of Biocultural Science for Revealing Costs of Social Goals and Facilitating Their Accomplishment

Biocultural science may eventually serve a function similar to that of an airline ticket office. It may be of little or no help in telling us where we ought to go, but it may help us estimate the costs of getting there and help us to make the journey.

This potential practical application of evolutionary biology has been illustrated by Charles Lumsden and Edward O. Wilson.[43] They used a fanciful social program involving the promotion of brother-sister incest because the scenario they drew was supported by a substantial amount of empirical evidence. The science involved in the exercise is, thus, quite solid. It is the social goal that is fantasized. The unreal flavor of the illustration was probably fortuitous because it makes it apolitical in that no ideologist of any stripe is likely at present to seriously consider the program described. But ideologists of the left, right, and center should see in the illustration how evolutionary biology has the potential for better informing them of the human costs of contemplated social programs and assisting them in the accomplishment of predetermined goals.

Before I describe the Lumsden and Wilson exercise, we should, by way of background, briefly look at the learning on incest avoidance which chapter V will cover more fully. There appears to be a specific genetic mechanism operating in humans that makes them averse to having sexual relations with anyone of the opposite sex with whom they were raised during a crucial period of childhood. Data from Israel and China provide strong evidence of this. In the Israeli kibbutzim, unrelated children were raised together communally. In the Chinese *sim pua* marriage situation, unrelated children were betrothed as youngsters and then raised together in the same household. In both of these situations, the children, as adults, had an aversion to sexual involvement with each other. In neither situation was there any societal opposition to such unions.

The Lumsden and Wilson exercise begins with an assumption that authoritative elements in society have decided to promote brother-sister unions in order symbolically to complete a unification process that began with their common ancestry—or for some other idealistic reason. A logical first step in achieving such a goal would be to remove the existing laws prohibiting brother-sister unions and take other appropriate steps to dissipate the cultural taboo against such unions. But that would not be sufficient to accomplish the goal. In the Chinese *sim pua* marriage and Israeli kibbutz situations there was no official or unofficial objection to the unions, yet the people who were raised together as youngsters were averse to them.

Here is where a knowledge of genetic programming as it responds to differing environments comes into the picture to facilitate the hypothesized program. Lumsden and Wilson suggest the genetic mechanism that works to make one averse to sexual relations with early childhood associates can be tricked in respect to brothers and sisters by raising them separate from one another, at least during the crucial early childhood years. That should remove the aversion and make brothers and sisters as sexually attractive to one another as they are to any other person with whom they were not raised as youngsters. However, they would not yet *prefer* each other, which is the goal of our hypothesized social planners.

At this point, culture comes back into the picture. To complete the total effort by having brothers and sisters prefer each other, Lumsden and Wilson suggest a cultural program romanticizing brother-sister unions in art, music, and literature.

But there are hidden costs in all this. Lumsden and Wilson bring the exercise up short by pointing out that an increase in unions between genetic brothers and sisters would result in a corresponding increase in the birth of stillborn or defective offspring due to the inbreeding depression phenomenon.[44] This may well be judged an unacceptable cost of the program. The authors go on to speculate that societal attitudes toward the plight of the affected offspring might be altered, just as the attitude of brothers and sisters toward each other might be altered, through a knowledge of evolutionary biology. That, however, would involve launching another program with economic and societal disruption and other costs that, when added to similar costs involved in the basic brother-sister union program, could prove to be unacceptable.

Would the goal facilitation and cost estimation uses of evolutionary biology suggested by the Lumsden and Wilson exercise have "normative" overtones? Not in the primary dictionary sense of indicating "principles of right action" or that "something ought to be done."[45] The goal facilitation use would, however, offer information that would arguably fit into a looser dictionary definition of "norm," as something that has "value."[46] If a goal has been decided upon, evolutionary biology may show social conditions that, if created, would be valuable in achieving the goal.

Similarly, the suggested cost estimation use of evolutionary biology would feed into social planning at the point where what has been defined as "normative science" is *arguably* being exercised by social planners. Normative science is said to be "a science that tests or evaluates and not merely describes or generalizes facts."[47] The cost estimation use of evolutionary biology would be introduced into the social planning process at the point where tentative goals are tested or evaluated prior to being finalized.[48] *But,* what social planners would take from natural science, and use in the evaluation process, is facts about the root causes of behavior and factual information on, or estimates of, human costs. The "logic, ethics, and aesthetics"[49] needed to make tentative and ultimate goal choices would have to be found elsewhere.

NOTES

1. See, in particular, Beckstrom, *Sociobiology and the Law.*
2. Ibid., 8.
3. Ibid., 76.
4. See Schwartz, "On the Prospects of Using Sociobiology in Shaping the Law: A Cautionary Note," 20: "The propensity of law to be guided by public opinion does not mean that the mores do in fact play a large part in shaping the law. While that relationship may be fundamental in primitive societies, as suggested by Bohannon . . . , public opinion offers much less guidance in urban societies because such societies are so normatively heterogeneous. . . . Recourse to science as a basis for nor-

mative judgment may reflect the need for some sort of consensus which is so lacking in our pluralistic, anomic society."

5. Ibid.
6. See, e.g., Alexander, *Darwinism and Human Affairs*, 270–71.
7. Reactions of this kind can be found in Lewontin, Rose, and Kamin, *Not in Our Genes*, 6, 9, 233–64, and Sociobiology Study Group of Science for the People, "Sociobiology—Another Biological Determinism" 280–90.
8. E. O. Wilson, *Sociobiology: The New Synthesis*.
9. E.g., Dawkins, *The Selfish Gene*; Barash, *Sociobiology and Behavior*; E. O. Wilson, *On Human Nature*; Alexander, *Darwinism and Human Affairs*.
10. Compare Lumsden and Wilson, *Promethean Fire*, 152, with Kitcher, *Vaulting Ambition*, 390.
11. See Alexander's speculation on responses to cultural situations based on normative ethics of "yesterday" in Alexander, *Darwinism and Human Affairs*, 271.
12. See Pfeiffer, *The Emergence of Society*, 33.
13. Alexander, *Darwinism and Human Affairs*, 90, 95, and Lumsden and Wilson, *Promethean Fire*, 182.
14. Alexander, *Darwinism and Human Affairs*, 93, 136–37, 277, and Lumsden and Wilson, *Promethean Fire*, 174.
15. See Lopreato, *Human Nature and Biocultural Evolution*, 70–71, and Dawkins, *The Selfish Gene*, 3.
16. Alexander, *Darwinism and Human Affairs*, 143, 277, and Beckstrom, "The Potential Dangers and Benefits of Introducing Sociobiology to Lawyers," 1282–83. Cf. Singer, *The Expanding Circle*, 131: "The growth of modern contraceptive techniques is a splendid example of the use of reason to overcome the normal consequences of our evolved behavior. It shows that reason can master our genes." It has been speculated that the use of contraceptives could eventually be eliminated by natural selection, as it is nonadaptive. However, a *selective* use of contraception may result in *optimal* reproduction in particular environments. In any event, Singer is surely right that the use of contraception by an individual short-circuits, on an ad hoc basis, whatever ancient genetic programming is pushing humans to copulate and thereby reproduce. For further observations on the same topic see van den Berghe, *Human Family Systems: An Evolutionary View*, 182–83.
17. Lumsden and Wilson, *Promethean Fire*, 182. Cf. the following statement by Sarah Blaffer Hrdy in *The Woman that Never Evolved*, 14–15: "[I]f social inequality based on sex is a serious problem, and if we really intend to do something constructive about it, we are going to need a comprehensive understanding of its causes. I am convinced that we will never adequately understand the present causes of sexual asymmetry in our own species until we understand its evolutionary history in the lines from which we descend."
18. Alexander, *The Biology of Moral Systems*, 192.
19. Dawkins, *The Selfish Gene*, 215. Cf. Barash, *The Whisperings Within*, 200:

"[I]t is unlikely that we are completely free." See also Breuer, *Sociobiology and the Human Dimension*, 263: "For what reasons does Dawkins *wish* 'to build a society in which individuals co-operate generously and unselfishly towards a common good,' if it is true that such a desire is in contradiction to his inborn human nature?" For possible answers to Breuer's question, see generally Alexander, *The Biology of Moral Systems*.

20. Dawkins, *The Selfish Gene*, 215.
21. Alexander, *The Biology of Moral Systems*, 109.
22. See Flew, "From Is to Ought," 146-47. See also Ruse, *Taking Darwin Seriously*, 78.
23. Morris, *Evolution and Human Nature*, 50-51. See also Edel, "Attempts to Derive Definitive Moral Patterns from Biology," 111, 112.
24. See Edel, "Attempts to Derive Definitive Moral Patterns," 112-13, for the following passage, published in 1955, many years before the emergence of the sociobiological synthesis: "To be rooted in a biological mechanism serving a biological need seems to many to be all the justification human behavior can ultimately ask. In this way, eating and drinking and sexual activity are obviously sanctioned. A variety of other invariant human tendencies, it is believed, will be found similarly to rest on more subtle biological mechanisms and thus prove their merit. Any institution claiming roots in instinct can thus clothe itself with the moral authority of absolute fixity. The history of social psychology is strewn with the wreckage of instincts intended to support prevalent institutional forms, such as pugnacity instincts to prop up war, acquisitive instincts to reinforce private property, and a variety of specific instincts to support the family."

   For a detailed effort to bring both utilitarianism and Kantianism into mutual focus with "Darwinism," see Ruse, *Taking Darwin Seriously*, 235–50.
25. For a discussion of the "naturalistic fallacy," as viewed by David Hume, Edward Moore and other philosophers, see Ruse, *Taking Darwin Seriously*, 86–93, and Maxwell, *Human Evolution*, 232–33. Albert Einstein said that "[a]s long as we remain within the realm of science proper, we can never meet with a sentence of the type 'thou shalt not.' . . . Scientific statements of facts and relations . . . cannot produce ethical directives" (Einstein, *Out of My Later Years*, 114).
26. Cf. the following quotation from *Biophilia*, in which author Edward O. Wilson took off his scientist's cap and expressed his personal feelings as a conservationist: "For if the whole process of our life is directed toward preserving our species and personal genes, preparing for future generations is an expression of the highest morality of which human beings are capable" (121).
27. See Barash, *The Whispering Within*, 234: "There is, of course, the danger that sociobiology will become something of a 'self-fulfilling prophecy,' an idea that influences our behavior because it predicts certain tendencies. But, if this happens, it will be a misuse of evolution, reflecting the

mistaken notion that what is, is necessarily good, and that what is, must be."

28. Alexander, *Darwinism and Human Affairs*, 138–39. But see Alexander, *The Biology of Moral Systems*, 166.

29. See Murphy, *Evolution, Morality, and the Meaning of Life*, 100: "The view of reason adopted by sociobiology is Humean and regards it as an *instrument* that allows us to calculate the best means to the attainment of our ends. It can even evaluate ends where these are seen as subordinate to even higher or more important ends. What it cannot do, however, is evaluate the ends finally accepted as ultimate, for these are given by the passions and, at this level, reason is the slave of the passions. And where do these basic passions come from? Evolutionary biology surely has, at least, part of the answer to this question."

30. E. O. Wilson, *On Human Nature*, 198.

31. Ibid.

32. See Lumsden and Wilson, *Promethean Fire*, 182–83: "[T]he philosophers and theologians have not yet shown us how the final truths will be recognized as things apart from the idiosyncratic development of the human mind. In the meantime, by appealing to the core principles of neurobiology, evolutionary theory, and cognitive science, practitioners of a new human science can reach a deeper understanding of why we feel certain courses of action to be intrinsically correct."

33. See ibid., 183: "For now . . . scientists can offer no guidance on whether we are really correct in making certain decisions, because no way is known to define what is *correct* without total reference to the moral feelings under scrutiny." See also Alexander, *The Biology of Moral Systems*, 220: "[N]o [solution of moral issues arises] out of evolutionary understanding. But perhaps our view of the issues can be clarified and our collective response as a result altered—and perhaps in a direction likely to be judged by those concerned as positive.

34. Alexander, *Darwinism and Human Affairs*, 278; Lumsden and Wilson, *Promethean Fire*, 183. See also Konner, *The Tangled Wing*, 180; Barash, *The Whisperings Within*; Breuer, *Sociobiology and the Human Dimension*, 73–76; and Murphy, *Evolution, Morality, and the Meaning of Life*.

35. Alexander, *Darwinism and Human Affairs*, 220. Kitcher, in an in-depth critique of sociobiology endorsed on the dustcover by the two best-known critics of the discipline, Richard Lewontin and Stephen Jay Gould, gives his approval to this use of the natural sciences (Kitcher, *Vaulting Ambition*, 420).

36. Alexander, *Darwinism and Human Affairs*, 276.

37. Ibid., 277. See also Ruse, *Taking Darwin Seriously*, 271: "Through social and genetic manipulation, our whole moral sense could be altered." But see Alexander, *The Biology of Moral Systems*, 256: "If we wish to create some particular kind of society—one that is different from that predicted from evolutionary history—then to know how to do it may well be

possible only by understanding that information from biology, and lots of it, must be included."

38. E. O. Wilson, *On Human Nature*, 196. See also Ruse and Wilson, "Moral Philosophy as Applied Science," 192.
39. Alexander, *Darwinism and Human Affairs*, 279–80.
40. Alexander, *The Biology of Moral Systems*, 11.
41. At the time of this writing the recognized world record for a mile was 3 minutes, 46.32 seconds (*Chicago Tribune*, July 3, 1987, §4, at 7, cols. 1 and 2).
42. See text of chapter I between note superscripts 10 and 12.
43. Lumsden and Wilson, *Promethean Fire*, 175–80.
44. See text at note superscript 19 in chapter V regarding inbreeding depression.
45. *Webster's Third New International Dictionary of the English Language*, s.v. "norm."
46. Ibid.
47. *Webster's*, s.v. "normative science."
48. Cf. Quinton, "Ethics and the Theory of Evolution," 139-40: "It would be widely agreed that evolutionary biology, by contributing to our knowledge about the consequences of action, can have an important subsidiary place in the rational formation of moral convictions. . . . Allowing . . . that the consequences of an action are relevant to its moral quality, we may admit that evolutionary knowledge, by giving us a new idea of the results to which conventionally approved lines of conduct will lead, may require the critical revision or development of these conventional approvals."
49. *Webster's*, s.v. "normative science."

Chapter
IV

Using Sociobiology to Expose Optional Solutions of Legal Problems

Introduction

In this chapter I want to explore yet another benefit that sociobiology might provide to legal systems—another way it might assist in the solution of social problems that work their way into legal arenas. This potential involves the provision of information concerning human behavior that might better illuminate practical problems and thereby expose optional solutions that would otherwise remain unseen. The type of information I refer to would grow out of the following proposition, which is no longer seriously disputed among the knowledgeable in the scientific community: human behavior is, to some extent, influenced by genetic programming.[1] Any disputes that now exist in this area of science can be reduced to questions of the manner and degree to which human behavior is genetically influenced.

When it is established that a given bit of behavior is genetically influenced to some degree, some degree of predictability will infuse the behavior. Eye blinking, for instance, seems quite clearly to be genetically influenced.[2] People are born with the trait. Thus when objects are thrust in people's faces, they will *normally* blink. Similarly, if sociobiological hypotheses regarding kin selection are correct, aid-giving behavior is genetically influenced so that when people can either aid their child or their mother, but not both, they will *typically* choose their child.[3]

This kind of behavioral predictability due to evolved genetic programming that today's humans may all have could eventually provide much information that will throw light on socio-legal problems. The illumination provided by science may seldom reveal clear solutions to such problems—indeed, it may serve to make the problem analyses more complex. But those analyses will be more appropriate because of the added insights accompanying the complexity. To illustrate the analytical mechanics I have in mind, and before we move to a human socio-legal problem, let me construct a comparatively simple problem involving human conflict with another species. The illustration involves animal behavioral study, but not evolutionary biology per se, and would not likely find its way into a legal arena.

Assume a problem arises in a human community surrounded by forests. Several people have been bitten seriously by members of a species of wild four-legged animals. The problem is how to resolve this interspecies conflict. Is the danger to humans so great that some collective action should be taken against the animals? Should the animals be eliminated from the vicinity of the human habitats? Value judgments would be involved in the ultimate solution to such a problem. Science cannot supply the involved values, but it might provide facts that can make the problem analysis more sophisticated and indicate a broader range of optional solutions. For example, assume now that a researcher on animal behavior produces a reliable study showing that the animal doing the biting virtually always attacks humans only when cornered, with no escape route. With that information the problem analysis becomes more complex, and a new question arises: can humans be educated to avoid cornering these animals, thus sufficiently alleviating the problem posed without sacrificing either human safety or the animals?

The information on animal behavior in this example was relatively straightforward. The researcher may have had no hypothesis regarding the circumstances under which the animal in question would attack. The animal may have simply been observed in encounters with other species and seen running away from humans when escape was possible and attacking when it was not. On the other hand, the researcher may have approached the research with a hypothesis along these lines—that another species as large as humans was not likely to be a food source for the animal, so attack on humans was likely to be a defense mechanism employed when fleeing was impossible.

Similar behavioral hypotheses, based on more complex conceptual roots, can be derived from sociobiological theory and prompt research that could provide factual information appropriate for helping solve the interhuman conflict problems with which the law must deal. In the remainder of this chapter I will illustrate this potential in a problem area involving child support collection through the legal system.

The sociobiological hypotheses I see as relevant to this legal problem concern paternity confidence and its effect on solicitude toward children. Researchers have found support for those hypotheses in ethnographic literature—reports describing various cultures of the world. This, and other pertinent data that may be forthcoming, could eventually provide information about paternity behavior that would suggest a new and different approach to the problem of collecting child support from men who have been adjudged to be fathers of children born out-of-wedlock.

Child Support Payments and Paternity Confidence

The collection of court-ordered child support payments has been a perennial problem in the United States.[4] It is just one aspect of the overall problem of the support of children in single-parent households,[5] but it is an aspect that has worked its way into the legal process. Elaborate judicial and administrative machinery has been set up by state and federal authorities to assist in the collection of delinquent child support. Some of this apparatus is of questionable efficiency: it may cost more money than it collects,[6] and, in spite of the apparatus, the nonpayment rate remains high.[7] Authorities concerned with child support payments should be receptive to any new idea that might increase the amount of child support that is voluntarily paid, particularly if the idea promises to be cost-effective. The seeds of such an idea may exist in evolutionary biology. Before getting into that, let us look a bit more at the legal system that leads to child support orders.

Child support orders can issue from a court during the dissolution of a marriage. They can also arise at the culmination of a paternity suit brought by a mother against the alleged father of her child, and this is the type upon which we will focus.[8] As a preliminary to a child support order in paternity suit proceedings, there will be a judgment rendered that the defendant is, in the eyes of the law, the father of the child. Various types of evidence may be accepted in court on the issue of whether the defendant is the father. At one time this evidence usually consisted of nothing more than the declaration of the mother that the defendant was the father and the defendant's admission or denial, together with whatever circumstantial evidence he could gather supporting the denial.[9] But several years ago the rules of these contests began to change when courts started accepting blood tests bearing on the question of whether the defendant was the father of the child.

For a time, the results of blood tests performed on samples from the three principals was only admitted, if at all, when the tests definitely excluded the defendant from paternity. For example, in the case of the basic ABO blood groups, a child of group AB blood can have an A, B, or AB parent, but cannot have a group O parent.[10] If the defendant proved to have group O blood, the courts would admit that evidence on the issue of whether he was the father. Science has said that if the test was conducted properly, he could not be the father. On the other hand, if the mother had group A blood, the child had group B, and the defendant had group B, the evidence would not be admitted. In this case, the test results indicate that the defendant *could* be the father—but, on that basis, so could millions of other men in the world.[11] Authorities have been reluctant to admit such inclusionary blood test evidence, as opposed to exclusionary blood test evidence, for fear that the "triers of fact"—juries or judges—would give more weight to the evidence than it is entitled to receive. But attitudes are changing regarding "inclusionary" evidence, mostly because blood testing is becoming increasingly sophisticated. Whereas at one time a defendant might be shown by blood tests to be included with many millions of other men having blood characteristics compatible with paternity of a given child, today he might be shown to be included with only a few thousand others—in the world, not just in the mother's community.

At the time this book was written, considerable publicity was being given to a new identification procedure called "DNA fingerprinting."[12] The test can be conducted on any type of tissue. It has been reported that "the chances of even siblings having identical DNA fingerprints (except for identical twins, who have the same genes) are estimated at 1 in 10 trillion."[13] If that is so, then presumably under ideal testing conditions, scientists could report that a given man is *almost certain* to be the *only* man who could have fathered a given child.[14]

Before DNA fingerprinting appeared on the scene, experts had said that the day was close when testing would be able to produce reports with a 99.8% probability, for example, that a defendant is the father of a child.[15] With DNA fingerprinting, the probabilities in a positive report should be considerably higher even than that. Unfortunately, there are a number of obstacles to such reports being generally available and useable in court. There are problems with deciding how probabilities are to be determined and interpreted to the triers of fact or other interested parties,[16] and there are problems with ensuring the reliability of testing procedures.[17] Also, testing can be quite costly, but test costs should decrease as testing procedures become more prevalent and standardized.[18] As the various problems are ironed out, inclusive paternity test results should become increasingly useful, and used, as evidence on the issue of the defendant's paternity in paternity lawsuits. Of course, in the meantime the system can function, as it traditionally has, relying on whatever other evidence is available. This may result in a certain amount of indifference or foot-dragging in the legal community with respect to the promotion of efforts to develop the testing and reporting of inclusive blood and tissue tests for paternity.[19] If another use for inclusionary information by the legal process were identified, it might prompt authorities to encourage a more rapid development of the techniques necessary to make such information more uniformly reliable and effectively useable in the legal process. Here is where sociobiology, and empirical research following its leads, come in.

Sociobiological theory suggests that men who could be assured through testing of a high degree of probability that they are the fathers of children would *typically* be more inclined to honor child support orders entered against them than men who did not receive such assurance. And the positive effect on payment could be especially effective in the cases of children conceived out of wedlock, as paternity doubt would normally be greater in those instances than in the cases where children are conceived when the men in question are married to the children's mothers. I referred briefly in chapter I to the sociobiological theory that relates to this paternity doubt issue.[20] We should look at it more fully now.

We have enough theoretical background from earlier chapters to start here with the proposition that humans are genetically programmed to render whatever aid they can to those with whom they have a high degree of genetic overlap in preference to comparative strangers, everything else being equal. Likewise, people are inclined to render aid to young genetic relatives in preference to old ones. The combination of these two inclinations would reach its highest expression in the attitude of parents toward their own children up to and including the early years of the children's maturity. If the initial parental generative investment is to reach fruition, the children must reach maturity able to be self-sustaining and, in turn, reproduce and nurture.

This particularized solicitude of adults for children hinges on the adults identifying the children as their own. It is generally accepted by scientists, at present, that humans have no innate or automatic mechanism by which they identify relatives, including offspring.[21] We apparently gather the identifying information from our environment. A male parent's identifying information may come from such clues as physical characteristics of the child that are similar to his and, especially, the mother's attribution of the child to him. A female is given more concrete evidence of her parenthood when she observes the child emerging from her womb. Therefore, sociobiologists conclude that men almost always can have less confidence that children are theirs than women can.[22]

When a mother attributes her child to a man, circumstances will exist that make the attribution more or less convincing to the man. As a generalization, it has to be the case that men who are said to be the fathers of children born to women to whom they were not married at the time of conception will have less paternity confidence, on the average, than men who were. There is an add-on effect working here because even the men married to the mothers, as we have noted, have less basis for confidence in their parenthood than the mothers do.

Sociobiological principles suggest that paternity doubt in a man will tend to have a negative effect, consciously or unconsciously, on the solicitude of the man toward a child attributed to him.[23] And there is corresponding empirical evidence suggesting that male solicitude toward attributed children correlates with males' perception of the probability that they are the fathers of the children.

This empirical evidence has been extracted by sociobiologists from ethnographic literature. They have noted that in several societies where promiscuity has been reported to be quite high and paternity confidence generally quite low, the men have tended to shift their solicitude from children attributed to them to their sisters' children.[24] The sociobiological explanation for such a shift of solicitude is that in a promiscuous society where paternity doubt is rife, the confidence a man can have that he and his sister share the same mother and that his sister's children are really hers looms large in his conscious or unconscious calculations regarding aid-giving.

In any case, the ethnographic literature lends some support to the sociobiological hypothesis that when paternity confidence is low, male genetic reproductive activity will tend to shift away from nurture of attributed children toward other pursuits that further the reproduction of their genes such as the nurture of youngsters with whom confidence of considerable genetic overlap is higher and continuing attempts to be responsible for pregnancies. Such activities create a call on whatever material resources the man has available.[25] Thus, if the hypothesis is correct, one can expect that American men against whom a paternity judgment has been rendered, followed by a child support decree, would *typically* be less inclined to honor the decrees than men subject to such decrees in respect to children conceived while they were married to the mothers.

This proposition, incidentally, should be testable by a study of support payments by men subject to "in-wedlock" child support orders compared to payments by those subject to "out-of-wedlock" child support orders. I know of no such study to date.[26]

Continuing to pursue the legal problem from a sociobiological perspective, our question now becomes: can anything be done to increase the paternity confidence of men subject to "out-of-wedlock" child support decrees to increase, in turn, their voluntary obedience to the decrees? My answer is: authorities should consider showing the men blood or tissue test results that indicate to a high degree of probability that they are the fathers of the children. As we have noted, for the first time in the history of humankind, this kind of evidence, produced by the cultural environment, may soon be generally available to add to the other types of environmental clues that men have historically had available.

If and when the probability of paternity tests and the procedures for reporting them become perfected and generally utilized to inform defendants in paternity proceedings, it is anyone's guess, at this point, how much of an effect such information would have on the honoring of child support orders. But it is certainly possible that, as testing procedures become more economical, increased collections would outweigh the costs of the procedure so as to make such paternity information programs cost-effective. And one should not lose sight of the fact that the test results could be used, simultaneously, to make more accurate and equitable the paternity decrees that precede the child support orders.

Further, if such a paternity information program were instituted, it could provide the opportunity for behavioral information to be fed back to scientists. If a foundation study were done soon to establish the level at which men subject to "out-of-wedlock" and "in-wedlock" child support decrees, respectively, are honoring the decrees, and a follow-up study were done at some date after the "out-of-wedlock" paternity information program was well established, behavioral scientists should be interested to see if the two categories of men drew closer together in the extent of their voluntary honoring of child support orders. If they did, the study could provide some support for sociobiological hypotheses.

I hope this illustration of the use of sociobiological theory, and research following its leads, to expose optional solutions to legal problems will stimulate others to search in sociobiology, on the one hand, and legal problem areas, on the other, to locate similar examples. In my efforts to relate sociobiology to the solution of legal problems I have been continually aware of my personal limitations. I feel like a traveler entering unexplored territory who has expertise in, say, insects and reptiles, but only a cursory familiarity with other fauna and flora. As others with more in-depth knowledge of the various specialized areas of the law become familiar with sociobiology, they will undoubtedly identify a large number of other instances where sociobiology might provide useful ideas to lawmakers.

NOTES

1. Cf. the following observation was made by Phillip Kitcher in *Vaulting Ambition* (1985), a book endorsed by the most distinguished critics of sociobiology: "The challenge for the sociobiologist is to continue the imaginative, but critical, work that is found in the best studies. . . . Some [animal] behavioral traits have evolutionary histories, and it is worthwhile to attempt to fathom them" (135).
2. See Konner, *The Tangled Wing*, 78.
3. See text of chapter I, supra, between note superscripts 17 and 21.
4. See generally Krause, *Child Support in America: The Legal Perspective.*
5. See generally Cassetty, ed., *The Parental Child-Support Obligation.*
6. See Krause, *Child Support in America*, 422–31.
7. See Lieberman, *Child Support in America*, 11: "Of the 4 million women who were owed child support in 1981, only 47 percent received the full amount due, and 28 percent received absolutely nothing; the aggregate amount of child support payments due in 1981 was $9.9 billion, but only $6.1 billion was actually received." See also Sorenson and MacDonald, "An Analysis of Child-Support Transfers," 41.
8. "In 1978, the [new federal program aimed at augmenting the collection of child support] located 453,620 absent fathers and established paternity in 110,714 cases. By 1983, those numbers had risen to 830,758 and 209,024, respectively. . . . The number of children born out of wedlock and living out of wedlock [in the U.S.] soared from 527,000 in 1970 to . . . 2,800,000 in 1982" (Lieberman, *Child Support in America*, 8).
9. See Krause, *Family Law Cases and Materials*, 448.
10. Schatkin, *Disputed Paternity Proceedings*, §5.02.
11. Ibid.
12. Chicago Tribune, Mar. 6, 1988, §5, p. 1, col. 2.
13. Ibid., p. 7, col. 3.
14. The president of Cellmark Diagnostics, a Germantown, Md., biotechnical concern, has said that DNA fingerprinting "can be used to determine

paternity of a child 'without doubt,' and is the first 'yes-no' test of paternity that has been developed" (in 13 *Fam. L. Rep.* 1567 [1987]).

15. See Krause, *Child Support in America*, 241. "With *further* scientific advances, especially in the HLA [human leucocyte antigens system] sector, the time may come . . . when the father of a child can be identified positively through medical expertise" (214).

See also Wilson, "Impact of the Uncertainty of Paternity on Family Law," 234–37.

16. Krause, *Child Support in America*, 226.

17. Ibid., 216.

18. Ibid., 245–46.

19. Ibid., 214.

20. See text of chapter I, supra, between note superscripts 18 and 19.

21. See note 20 to chapter I.

22. See note 19 to chapter I.

23. Barash, *Sociobiology and Behavior*, 319, and Daly and Wilson, *Sex, Evolution, and Behavior*, 167. See also Alexander, *Darwinism and Human Affairs*, 174–75.

24. Alexander, *Darwinism and Human Affairs*, 169–75; Kurland, "Paternity, Mother's Brother, and Human Sociality," 157–67; Irons, "Investment and Primary Social Dyads," 184–92; Gaulin and Schlegel, "Paternal Confidence and Paternal Investment: A Cross-Cultural Test of a Sociobiological Hypothesis." See Symons, *The Evolution of Human Sexuality*, 244, where the author notes a society in which there did not appear to be a correlation between paternity uncertainty and investment in sisters' children. But see Irons, 209–13, regarding the variety of other environmental factors that could intercede in the equation while being consistent with the kin selection hypothesis (see text of chapter I between note superscripts 11 and 15 and the relevant notes).

25. See Barash, *Sociobiology and Behavior*, 318.

26. In a comprehensive empirical study of the payment patterns of men subject to child support orders in a Michigan county, the researchers included a sample of men ordered to pay whose orders arose from paternity actions, but the report does not compare the payment record of those men with those whose orders arose out of divorce actions (Chambers, *Making Fathers Pay*, 71–162, 303, 304–34).

Limits on Using Sociobiology in Lawmaking: Undetectable Genetic Input to Behavior

Introduction

In chapter II we saw how sociobiology might assist lawmakers in their widespread efforts to assess typical human behavior. In the last chapter, I illustrated how sociobiological predictions concerning typical behavior might reveal optional solutions to socio-legal problems. Here I will demonstrate how sociobiology may often, even when fully developed, fail to be of assistance in assessing or predicting typical behavior. That insight should serve as a caution, but also help us better appreciate the circumstances under which sociobiology *does* hold potential for predicting typical behavior. To the extent that biocultural learning allows for typical behavior prediction in human populations, that ability is based upon the relatively universal and constant genetic input to behavior that humans are presumed to possess because of evolutionary processes. On the other hand, to the extent that culture influences behavior, typical behavior becomes less predictable. This loss of predictability is due to the comparatively fluid and rapidly changing nature of cultural environments and the necessity that culture be learned to have an effect on behavior. For one reason or another, given individuals may never come into contact with a given bit of culture or, if they do, may not absorb its lessons.

This gene-culture distinction will prove to be important to lawmakers looking to science for information on typical behavior. Science might provide reasonable assurance that certain behavior typically may be expected to the extent that a substantial genetic input can be detected or presumed to exist. Conversely, to the extent that genetic input cannot be detected or presumed to exist, while cultural input can be, one is less entitled to expect the behavior in question from the group of individuals involved. In this chapter, I will use a current legal problem area to illustrate the proposition that biocultural science becomes less valuable to lawmakers interested in typical behavior as the genetic input to behavior becomes less detectable.

In a publication on the possible use of sociobiology in the solution of a legal problem, legal scholar John Oakley has asked if the discipline might eventually provide useful insights for lawmakers struggling with the issue of whether legally closed adoption records should be opened to adoptees seeking information about their birth (biological) parents.[1] Many U.S. jurisdictions will not provide such access if the adoptees give no other reason than a desire for self-identification or a psychological "need to know."[2]

Professor Oakley assumes that to the extent the search by adoptees for their birth families is "biologically" (genetically) prompted, the adoptees can be expected to suffer genuine emotional pain when frustrated in their searches. Further, he believes lawmakers should be interested in learning that such is the case. At the heart of the matter is genetically induced motivation. Oakley asks if processes of evolution have created in humans an "innate desire" (best interpreted as a strong extensive genetic, as opposed to environmental, input to human motivation)[3] to know their ancestry because to do so has had an adaptive advantage in that (1) incest avoidance is thus facilitated and/or (2) aid-giving exchanges are more profitable the closer the genetic relationship of the individuals involved in the exchanges. Oakley does not attempt to answer these two questions but suggests that others elaborate on his idea. I will attempt to do that here.

I believe Professor Oakley had a creditable thought. At an informal gathering I posed Oakley's questions to some anthropologists deeply steeped in evolutionary biology. They did not dismiss out of hand the implicit suggestions contained in his questions. These anthropologists are aware of the complexities of the learning surrounding evolutionary biology, its distinctly unsettled nature, and the need for a review of its relevant details before even a tentative answer should be given to questions like Oakley's.

I certainly am not offering the last word on these questions. However, my tentative conclusion, based upon the present state of knowledge in sociobiology, is that any common need of adoptees to know their ancestry is unlikely to have an extensive or strong genetic basis in the adoptees. Culturally (environmentally) induced impulses rather than genetically programmed impulses operating in the adoptees are likely to be the main factor behind any such need. A conclusion of this sort is valuable and instructive at this stage of the introduction of lawyers to evolutionary biology. We lawyers with a knowledge of sociobiology need to become sensitized to the fact that it will not always provide a direct genetic explanation for a bit of behavior. We also need to develop techniques for using biocultural learning in the analysis of legal problems. The exercise I will conduct in this chapter may help to develop such techniques.

I will first introduce the legal problem and the possible assistance that lawmakers grappling with it might derive from a knowledge of sociobiology. Then I will examine the relevant theoretical and empirical evidence developed by scientists that led me to my tentative conclusion.

The Legal Problem

Many U.S. jurisdictions provide that court records concerning an adoption, and the original birth certificate containing names and other identifying characteristics of the birth parents, can be sealed and made unavailable to the public upon the request of a party to the adoption proceedings.[4] The principal applicants for access to closed records are adoptees who have attained adulthood. Normally an applicant can obtain access to the records only if "good cause" is shown to a court. Various reasons have been accepted as "good cause" for access, including physical health problems and certified psychotic disorders that might be solved by locating close biological family members.[5] However, the courts have quite uniformly refused access by adoptees who have not had specific, cogent reasons. Adoptees have generally been unsuccessful if they have simply had "a desire to discover [their] natural identity."[6] The collective position of these adoptees has been variously stated by commentators who were attempting to combine statements of adoptees themselves and speculations of psychologists. The following is typical:

> Once an adopted child learns that he or she has two sets of parents, one biological and the other legal, the characteristic curiosity—"who am I?"—is heightened to an often psychically damaging degree. Even though the adoptive parents have been excellent parents by current standards, the child's genetic makeup is inalterably different from their own; a fact not lost on the child. Adopted children, particularly in adolescence, frequently experience feelings of rejection and insecurity following their realization of dual parentage. They may also be intensely interested in discovering the biological, psychological and socioeconomic characteristics of their birth parents in order to understand their own traits and to gain insights for predicting their future.[7]

Whatever the rhetoric used to describe the phenomenon, one must take notice of the *fact* that significant numbers of adult adoptees have had such an intense desire to locate, or at least identify, their biological family that they have been willing to spend large amounts of time and money toward that end.[8] They have, furthermore, formed organizations[9] for the purpose of convincing lawmakers to give them ready access to closed records containing the information they seek.[10] But the adoptees have met with organized resistance to their efforts. Organizations of adoption agencies, adoptive parents, and people generally interested in the welfare of children argue for closed adoption records or, at least, for limited types of access calculated to protect the birth families from unwanted contact by adoptees.[11] The position of these groups reflects the philosophy behind the enactment of laws that provide for closed adoption records. It has been said that closed records help to preserve the integrity of the adoption process, which is a "humane solution to the serious social problem of children who are or may become unwanted, abused or neglected."[12] For the adoption process to work smoothly, it is important to have a supply of capable adoptive parents and to have birth parents who look favorably on the adoption process.

Adoptive parents tend to like the sealed records system, apparently for the effect it might have in insulating them from loss of love and contact with the adopted child that might occur when the child, at adulthood, makes contact with the birth family.[13] It has been suggested that without this ensurance of insulation, fewer capable prospective adoptive parents would actually adopt.[14]

The position of birth parents in the adoption triangle has been largely voiced by others. The birth parents are not very vocal or well organized, for fairly obvious reasons.[15] For a large percentage of these parents, the children represent mistakes made early in their lives. It would be an embarrassment, at least, and perhaps a severe disruption to their later lives, to have those mistakes revealed.[16] It has been argued that the ensurance of insulation through the closed records scheme can help to encourage birth parents to use the adoption process in lieu of other options, including abortion and abandonment of children after birth.[17] These are the types of arguments that lawmakers hear from the other side when contemplating requests by adoptees for access to their adoption records without having to show "good cause." As we noted earlier, Professor Oakley feels that weight may be added to the adoptees' side of the scale when balancing the considerations involved to the extent that adoptees (1) tend to suffer psychologically or emotionally when frustrated in attempts to identify and locate their birth families and (2) their desires in that regard are genetically induced.

I am willing to assume, with Professor Oakley, that lawmakers should know of any common psychogenic suffering that occurs among adoptees. Certainly relief of suffering is a concern of lawmakers, so the extent to which those involved in the adoption triangle suffer is a legitimate consideration in the issue of opening adoption records.

But at this point I have two problems with the rationale behind Professor Oakley's inquiry. The first involves a balancing of interests. I do not know how one can quantify the collective suffering, genetically based or otherwise, of adoptive and birth parents if adoptees are given unrestricted access to adoption records. Conceivably, one day science may provide means for such quantification and thereby permit such suffering to be weighed against the suffering by adoptees. But the means are not now available. My second problem, concentrating now only on the suffering of adoptees, involves the question of why discomfort, traceable to genetic programming in the sufferer, should be of more interest to lawmakers than discomfort that is the result of the sufferer's response to cultural influences. I know of no evidence that a person suffers less when frustrated in achieving a desire that has little or no basis in the person's genetic makeup but was induced primarily or exclusively by cultural messages. Assuming that the desire to identify parents and siblings does not reflect genetic programming of the adoptees—aside from some general programming prompting them to accommodate cultural messages such as the condemnation of incest—should lawmakers pay any less attention to genuine discomfort the adoptees suffer? I would suppose not. Thus I cannot see why the extent of genetic input to a desire to identify and locate birth families should matter *if* the adoptees are telling the truth when they say they suffer pain when frustrated in their quest. But that last proviso suggests a reason why I can stay with Professor Oakley and his inquiry. The existence of genetic input might help to establish the adoptees' credibility.

Lawmakers might be persuaded to *generally* open sealed records to adoptees if the lawmakers were given some assurance that virtually *all* adoptees who are frustrated in their quest will suffer appreciable psychological or emotional pain. The existence within the adoptees of a strong or extensive genetic basis for the "need to know" might help to provide that assurance. If "pure" culture[18] were the only operative factor, one would assume that some adoptees could have escaped its influence. On the other hand, if, and to the extent that, evolutionary processes have instilled in all humans a "need to know" their birth families, one may gain some assurance that none of the adoptees who search for their families are simply being idly curious. Evolved biology has a degree of reliability that environment and culture do not have. We can, for example, have more assurance that members of a Christian church were born with an appendix (though its absence would not be externally noticeable) than that they actually believe in the existence of God; and genetically influenced emotions, as opposed to body organs, should also have comparatively reliable manifestations throughout the population. Therefore, I see a possible practical benefit from an attempt to assess whether, and the extent to which, adoptees' "need to know" their birth family has a genetic basis.

Looking for Biocultural Origins of Adoptees' "Need to Know" Their Birth Families

Let us first deal with incest avoidance as an explanation of adult adoptees' search for their birth families. Later we will explore the possibility that a comparative reproductive "fitness" advantage from carrying on aid-giving exchanges and cooperative behavior in the midst of close genetic kin is behind such searches.

Trying to Avoid Incest

A keystone observation regarding incest avoidance is that close inbreeding appears to have serious negative consequences on the vitality of offspring (called "inbreeding depression").[19] This is particularly true in respect to matings between people related by one-half, that is, between siblings and between parents and their children.[20] Vitality of offspring is, of course, a crucial aspect of successful reproduction, so we should inquire as to the ways in which the selection process of evolution, which hinges on reproduction, may have taken inbreeding depression into account. We should be looking for mechanisms by which close inbreeding is avoided.

The most prominent biologically based[21] explanation of the mechanics of incest avoidance behavior in humans focuses on two sources. The first source is an apparent specific genetic mechanism that "negatively imprints" humans against having sexual relations with those with whom they were closely associated during a crucial span of their childhood years.[22] The second source is a cultural message often called the incest taboo.[23]

Some think that the incest taboo operates as a type of backstop to the negative imprinting. The intensity of the taboo may vary in inverse relation to the intensity of the negative imprinting in a given society. According to this hypothesis, negative imprinting will be relatively strong in a society that is permissive of such things as prepubertal children being nude in each other's presence and engaging in infantile sex play. With generally strong imprinting, there will be less need for backstopping by the taboo, so the latter will be weaker than in a society that is not so permissive.[24]

We should now note a critical distinction between the incest taboo and the negative imprint. The taboo is kin specific — at least in U.S. society, where the adoptees we have in focus reside. Here the message of the taboo is "Don't have sexual relations with a sibling, parent, etc." The negative imprint, however, is not kin specific. It leaves an individual with a disinclination to have sexual relations with people, kin or not, with whom the individual closely associated during a crucial period in childhood. There is empirical evidence that this negative imprinting operates in respect to early peers — other children. The possibility that the negative imprinting might similarly occur in a child in respect to associated adults — in particular, caretaking adults — is more purely speculative at present.[25]

The empirical evidence regarding peers comes primarily from two sources.[26] One is Israeli kibbutzim, where children are raised communally. Studies have indicated that unrelated adults raised together as children in the kibbutzim had an aversion to sexual relations with, and did not marry, one another even though public opinion was not opposed to such unions.[27] The second source is an institution that existed in some parts of China called *sim pua* marriage. This involved a form of marriage whereby a young girl would be adopted, often as an infant, by a family for the purpose of providing a wife for a young son of the family. The children were raised together. Researchers have reported a clear reluctance of the partners to consummate these marriages upon reaching adulthood.[28] Parental pressures forced couples to overcome their reluctance, but studies have shown that the reproductive rate in such unions was nearly one-third below the normal.[29] Furthermore, couples in these marriages had a considerably higher rate of extramarital sexual relations and a considerably higher rate of divorce than normal (24 percent versus 1.2 percent).[30]

If inbreeding depression — the loss of vitality in offspring when close genetic relatives mate — is the problem, why would the process of evolution have resulted in conditioning that prompts people to avoid sexual relations with those who were close associates in their early

years *regardless* of the genetic relationship? Why are humans not programmed through an evolved direct mechanism to avoid sexual relations with close genetic relatives specifically?

One answer that scientists have given us is based on the proposition that genetic programming which accomplishes a reproductively
beneficial result with the most neural economy, will be selected for and
prevail in the gene pool.[31] Theorists suggest that during the part of our
evolutionary past when the major part of our genetic programming
was set in place, small, relatively isolated social groups were the norm.
If a child was "adopted" into a nuclear family, the child was likely a
close genetic relative, such as a niece or nephew of one of the parents.[32]
Thus in order for people to be programmed in a neurally economical
fashion to avoid the most harmful types of incest, it was only necessary
that they have an aversion to sexual relations with persons living in
the same household. Any competing genetic program that gave individuals the more complex neural equipment necessary to distinguish
between genetic relatives and nonrelatives would have wasted energy
and been selected against in the evolutionary process.[33]

We should note here that some scientists have suggested a considerably different biological interpretation of the Israeli kibbutzim and
Chinese *sim pua* marriage data.[34] Under this view the avoidance of sex
with close associates from early years does not evidence a genetic
mechanism aimed at incest avoidance. Instead, it is a manifestation of
another type of fitness-enhancing reproductive programming, in males
at least.[35] This programming results in the "Coolidge effect," so named
because of an illustrative conversation that President Calvin Coolidge
supposedly had with a chicken breeder.[36] Behavior conforming to the
"Coolidge effect" has been observed in other animal species.[37] It involves individuals acting to maximize the number of sexual contacts
they have with different members of the other sex with the result that
the number and/or genetic variety of their offspring is maximized. This
programming would include a "fitness-enhancing taste for novelty."[38]
The flip side of that coin could be aversion to sexual relations with
those to whom one has become habituated. And that effect, it has been
suggested, might extend even to those with whom one associates in
early childhood.[39]

Even if the observed phenomenon of sexual aversion to early
associates is a manifestation of genetic programming to accomplish the
Coolidge effect, it may still have an *incidental* result of avoiding some
inbreeding depression to the extent that the people avoided happen
to be close genetic relatives. In any event, whether the phenomenon
of early associate avoidance is an incidental result of programming for

the Coolidge effect or the result of a neurally economical genetic mechanism that evolved in response to the inbreeding depression problem, it seems clear that the possible source of adoptees' "need to know" is not locatable in the phenomenon. Neither of the two explanations for the phenomenon encompasses a "need to know" the identity of close genetic relatives. If such a need exists in adoptees, theorization to date suggests we must look elsewhere to trace the source. And that shifts our focus to the other empirically observed phenomenon—the incest taboo.

It has often been claimed that incest taboos are universal in human societies, although the point seems debatable.[40] In any event, an incest taboo exists generally throughout the United States, where the adoptees in our focus reside. Sanctions applied in U.S. society include the legal prohibition of marriage between listed relatives and criminal penalties for such relatives who intermarry or have sexual intercourse with each other.[41] The relatives falling within these restrictions have quite generally in the past,[42] and in some states to date,[43] included in-laws, adoptive relatives, and step-relatives, as well as close genetic relatives. However, when states have become parsimonious in their listings, they have tended to include only very close genetic relatives[44]—those related by one-half, one-fourth, or one-eighth.[45]

It seems fair to say that most U.S. adults, if they do not know specifically about the legal restrictions, have at least been made aware that society frowns on sexual relations between children and their parents and between siblings and that offenders may suffer some kind of adverse consequence. The incest taboo, then, may be the first place that one should look to trace the origins of adult adoptees' desire to locate and identify their close genetic relatives, *assuming* that the motivation is incest avoidance.

Adoptees, with more or less conscious awareness of what they are doing, may be seeking to avoid societal sanctions. We should note that the societal message does not clearly include an excuse for those who marry or have sexual relations with close genetic relatives when the parties are unaware of the relationship.[46] I, for one am quite sure that if I were an adoptee I would like to be able to identify my close genetic relatives if I thought I could be prosecuted for marrying or having sexual relations with them when unaware of their identity. In a densely populated, fluid urban environment, the chances of my happening into a marriage or sexual encounter with one of my unidentified close kin and then later having someone discover the relationship and prosecute me may be slim—but I would rather not take the chance. Then there is the opprobrium I might suffer even if I am not prosecuted. My ruminations have become subjective, but objective information is lacking. Could actual adoptees be reacting to the threat of sanctions in somewhat the way I think I would? The chances that they could be seem good enough to entitle the incest taboo to most of our attention in this inquiry.

Our question, again, is *if* the effort of adoptees to identify close genetic relatives has a basis in *incest avoidance*, from where, more specifically, does the motivation derive? As the relatively specific genetic mechanisms that scientists have considered in the incest context do not seem to be the source, the incest taboo appears to be the best point of focus. That is not to suggest, however, that "pure" culture need be the complete, ultimate source of the motivation.

If sociobiologists were forced to label the incest taboo as *either* a biological *or* a cultural phenomenon, they would have to opt for "cultural."[47] But they prefer to call it something like "biocultural."[48] Sociobiologists believe that culture in this case is relatively loosely shaped, controlled and constrained by what some have called "epigenetic rules."[49] These are genetically coded rules for conduct that give us a general outline of what to do, but leave specifics up to selection by the actor from a range, or "band width," of possible responses that will be more or less appropriate depending upon the environmental circumstances the actor encounters.[50] Within such a framework a group of people may collectively create societally sanctioned rules of behavior that are fitness-enhancing for all, or at least some (perhaps the most dominant) members of the group.[51]

At this point let me record my thoughts on a possible biocultural, mechanistic explanation for the incest taboo. Up to now I have been able to cite authority for virtually every observation I have laid out. The following schematic, however, is to some extent my own construction from clues that sociobiologists have provided. In any case, it is not a necessary part of the tentative conclusions I make hereafter about the state of biocultural science as it bears on the legal questions we are addressing.

The incest taboo's interdiction of sexual relations between "parents" and their "children," between "siblings," etc., *specifically*, may reflect a progressive causal chain between (1) a precultural[52] negative imprinting against sexual relations with early childhood associates, (2) the perception and reasoning ability of humans to identify such associates as most often being in the birth family, (3) the affixing of descriptive labels from the cultural invention of language to birth family members so identified,[53] and (4) the use of the resulting cultural artifact (or "culturgen")[54] by some elements of society to serve their interests[55] as guided by their epigenetic programming.[56]

Let us return to our pursuit. At this point the issue is: Does the incest taboo reflect, to an appreciable extent, epigenetic programming operating in our adoptees, or is it principally or solely a reflection of epigenetic programming operating in other elements of the population for the benefit of those elements? If it is the latter, then we might conclude that if adoptees are following the dictates of the incest taboo when they seek out their birth families, they are being motivated primarily by cultural messages. I will now try to weave together clues that may help us to answer this question. Again I must caution the reader: we are in a particularly hazy and largely uncharted area, but we must do the best we can to give Professor Oakley an answer.

Societal leaders and rulemakers could have many and complex reasons for influencing the institution and maintenance of an incest taboo. Whatever their reasons, it is a good guess that at any given time the outlines of an incest taboo reflect the interests of those people as dictated by their epigenetic programming.[57] It is not as likely that the U.S. incest taboo also reflects the epigenetic programming of adoptees searching for their birth parents. The adoptee searchers tend to be young adults, not yet in a position to lead or make rules in society.[58] It is *possible* that they have different personal attitudes toward incest than the leaders and rulemakers, because they have more immediate interest in the reproductive consequences of it. The adoptees tend to be in the early part of their child-generating years,[59] whereas legal rulemakers, at least, tend to be beyond their child-generating years or in the later part of them.[60] This age difference could result in somewhat different attitudes toward incest, since epigenetic programming is said to call for varying responses as one's social environment and other circumstances change in the course of a lifetime.[61]

So we do not know whether the incest taboo reflects epigenetic programming operating in our adoptees. But we do know that our adoptees can feel the social effects of the incest taboo and are subject to its sanctions. If they have sexual relations with a birth family member they could be jailed for all they know. They, therefore, have incentive to pay attention to whatever explicit or implicit lessons are contained in the taboo.

Thus, *if* adoptees are acting to avoid incest when they search for their birth families, we can say at present that (1) it appears this is not due to a comparatively specific genetic mechanism, (2) we do not know whether the behavior reflects comparatively loose, nonspecific genetic (epigenetic) programming operating within the adoptees, but (3) we do see how it may be culturally induced.

This review of the scientific evidence concerning incest leads me to the tentative conclusion that the activity of U.S. adoptees in seeking to identify their birth family has little, if any, connection to genetic programming existing *in the adoptees* that is *aimed at incest avoidance.*[62] But that only answers one of Professor Oakley's two questions. Let us turn to the second.

Fitness Advantage of Interacting with Genetic Kin

Professor Oakley's second question can be rephrased now as follows: What is the extent of any genetic input to U.S. adoptees' drive to identify their birth families, *assuming* that the underlying goal is interacting with close genetic relatives in aid-giving exchanges? Initially, we should observe that there is no clear evidence here, as there is in regard to incest avoidance, of any relevant genetic and/or cultural mechanism. That is not to say that such a mechanism does not exist. But if it does, it is not so obvious as to have caught the attention of natural or social scientists.

As an abstract matter we can approach the question with an assumption upon which most sociobiologists would agree: historically there should have been a genetic reproductive fitness advantage for those who interacted with kin rather than non-kin, everything else being equal (such as the alternative groups with which the individual might have interacted having essentially equal resources). Cooperation and reciprocal aid-giving can be advantageous in themselves for any participant. But when the participants are closely related, cooperation[63] and reciprocal aid-giving are yet more fitness-enhancing than when the participants are not.[64] In respect to reciprocal aid-giving, there are said to be two reasons for this. First, "cheating" (giving less than a full return) by an individual and the consequent losses to another are less likely to occur between close genetic relatives than between comparative strangers because one gains less by cheating a relative than by cheating a comparative stranger, everything else being equal. Cheating in dealings with a relative is, in "genotypic" effect, cheating oneself— to the extent that one's genes overlap with those of that relative.[65] Second, if the other party fails to reciprocate for whatever reason, one's genetic complement can nevertheless benefit from the interaction to the extent that one's genes overlap with the other party's.[66]

Assuming that interacting with close relatives is fitness-enhancing, it nevertheless seems unlikely that there is any comparatively specific genetic mechanism that is prompting adoptees to seek to identify close relatives for the purpose of interacting with them. In the first place, anthropological evidence suggests that during the period of early human history during which, sociobiologists theorize, most of our genetic programming was set in place,[67] humans were settled in comparatively small, scattered, isolated groups.[68] Such conditions, *of themselves*, would have promoted the adhesion of kin groups. It is questionable whether any genetic programming specifically prompting interaction with close kin could have gained a significant advantage in the gene pool.[69]

Second, and more important, assuming such programming *would* have conferred a significant advantage in the group living conditions just described, the result could probably have been obtained by a more neurologically economical program that did not call for the identification of close genetic kin, but merely promoted interaction with people who happened to be around the individual in his or her early years.[70] Such early associates would almost always have been the individual's close relatives as a matter of course. We have already noted that similar comparatively specific, yet non–kin-specific, programming might appear to be operative in humans in respect to incest avoidance.[71]

Of course, simply because one genetic programming combination might theoretically achieve a result more economically than another does not mean that the economical one arose and prevailed in the gene pool. The initial appearance in the gene pool of genetic combinations appears to be quite random and accidental.[72] It is possible that a genetic combination for kin-specific programming fell into place at some point in human evolution and, meeting no competition from a more efficient program, prevailed in the gene pool. However, in the absence of clear evidence of *any* kind of program aimed at prompting interactions with kin, the best bet is that if any comparatively specific programming does exist today, it is not kin specific.

If that is true, and if adoptees have any genetically induced drive to locate their genetic kin so as to make their social interactions more fitness-enhancing, the origins of that drive must lie elsewhere. When we shift our focus to culture we see little of relevance. As we saw with incest avoidance, scientists have suggested that generalized epigenetic rules for fitness enhancement can lurk behind cultural messages. But if there is some sort of cultural message promoting aid-giving and cooperative interaction between close genetic kin, it is so obscure as to have escaped the notice of social commentators. Certainly there is nothing here as clear and forceful as the incest taboo. The closest cultural messages I can think of in U.S. society are the aphorisms "take care of your own," "charity begins at home," and "honor thy parents." These do not specify close genetic kin, have no appreciable sanctions behind them, and, in any case, are counterbalanced by "be kind to your neighbors."

Thus, neither scientific theory nor late twentieth-century U.S. culture provide clues which might suggest that U.S. adoptees' desire to locate and identify close genetic kin is motivated by even loose genetic programming aimed at promoting the aid-giving interaction of close genetic kin.

Conclusion

Significant numbers of adoptees upon reaching adulthood make efforts to locate and identify their birth families. Legal scholar John Oakley has asked whether this activity is motivated by some genetic programming in the adoptees that hinges on incest avoidance or the advantages of interacting with genetic kin. My answer is: If such genetic programming is there, I have found no biocultural scientific theory or empirical source that provides evidence of it.

No one would suppose that sociobiology will ultimately provide answers to every legal problem involving an analysis of human behavior. There is little doubt, however, that sociobiology could provide help in solving a great many such problems if and when the theory becomes well substantiated.[73] A present agenda for scholars straddling human behavior studies and the law is to map the areas where the potential benefits of evolutionary biology to the legal process exist. Such mapping will often call for employing scientific evidence in a detailed analysis of the sort I have tried to illustrate in this chapter.

NOTES

1. Oakley, "Sociobiology and the Law," 43.
2. Northwestern University Law Review Board of Editors, Comment, "Breaking the Seal: Constitutional and Statutory Approaches to Adult Adoptees' Right to Identity," 316.
3. See Alexander, "Biology and Law," 19–20. But see E. O. Wilson, *Sociobiology: The Abridged Edition*, 18-19, regarding acceptable usages of the terms "instinctive behavior" and "learned behavior," when carefully defined.
4. See generally Nw. U.L. Rev., Comment.
5. Ibid.
6. See, e.g., *In re Roger B.*, 84 Ill. 2d 323, 418 N.E.2d 751 (1981), appeal dismissed, 454 U.S. 806 (1981).

7. Katz, Introduction to J. Triseliotis, *In Search of Origins*, x.

8. A sample of forty adult adoptees in 1954 showed 50 percent had made some attempt to search for their birth parents, and another survey with a larger sample in 1975 and 1981 showed 20 percent of the adult adoptees asked their adoptive parents to see their birth record (Feigelman and Silverman, *Chosen Children*, 211–13, 224).

9. See Appendix to Sorosky, Baran, and Pannor, *The Adoption Triangle*, 227, for a list of such organizations around the United States, Canada, and Mexico.

10. See Pierce, "Survey of State Laws and Legislation on Access to Adoption Records—1983," where law reform activities of adoption-oriented organizations are summarized.

11. Ibid.

12. Klibanoff, "Genealogical Information in Adoption: The Adoptee's Quest and the Law," 186.

13. Sorosky, Baran, and Pannor, *The Adoption Triangle*, 38, 220–21, and Feigelman and Silverman, *Chosen Children*, 197.

14. Feigelman and Silverman, *Chosen Children*, 221.

15. But see ibid., 228. An organization called Concerned United Birthparents is listed as having branches in two Eastern states.

16. See ibid., 38, 219; *In re Roger B.*, 84 Ill. 2d 323, 329–30, 418 N.E.2d 751, 754 (1981); and *In re Maples*, 563 S.W.2d 760, 763 (Mo. 1978).

17. See Sorosky, Baran, and Pannor, *The Adoption Triangle*, 219, and Haimes and Timms, *Adoption, Identity and Social Policy*, 12–13.

18. It may be that *any* bit of behavior, in spite of apparent cultural trappings, is influenced to some extent by genetic programming of the actor *and* of those who collectively create the culture. See generally Lumsden and Wilson, *Promethean Fire* (1983) (essentially an "English" translation by the authors of their heavily mathematical book, *Genes, Mind, Culture*).

19. Shepher, *Incest: A Biosocial View*, 89-93, and van den Berghe, "Human Inbreeding Avoidance: Culture in Nature," 93.

20. See the authorities cited in note 19 supra and the empirical evidence in Seemanova, "A Study of Children of Incestuous Matings."

21. Sociological and psychological explanations for incest avoidance behavior with virtually no genetic orientation are reviewed by Shepher, *Incest: A Biosocial View*, 135–73. See also Lopreato, *Human Nature and Biocultural Evolution*, 315–16.

22. Van den Berghe, "Human Inbreeding Avoidance," 95–98. See also Shepher, *Incest: A Biosocial View*, 43–49.

23. Van den Berghe, "Human Inbreeding Avoidance," 98; "Attacking the Last Taboo," *Time*, Apr. 14, 1980, 72.

24. Van den Berghe, "Human Inbreeding Avoidance," 98.

25. Shepher, *Incest: A Biosocial View*, 110, 114–15, 119, and van den Berghe, "Human Inbreeding Avoidance," 96–97, 118.

26. See van den Berghe, "Human Inbreeding Avoidance," 96, regarding other sources.

27. Shepher, "Mate Selection among Second-Generation Kibbutz Adolescents and Adults: Incest Avoidance and Negative Imprinting."
28. Wolf and Huang, *Marriage and Adoption in China, 1845-1945,* 82.
29. Shepher, *Incest: A Biosocial View,* 65.
30. Ibid.
31. Symons, *The Evolution of Human Sexuality,* 18, and Alcock, *Animal Behavior,* 119–20.
32. See Barash, *Sociobiology and Behavior,* 313. See, more specifically, Lopreato, *Human Nature,* 319: "Humans have typically lived in societies of 25–30 individuals for most of their evolutionary history," and see Pfeiffer, *The Emergence of Society,* 33: "Band size . . . tends to hover around the 'magic number' of twenty-five . . . for Bushmen, Australian aborigines, and other present-day hunter-gatherers, and, according to estimates based on the areas of excavated living sites, for their prehistoric ancestors as well."

    Cf. Chagnon, "Terminological Kinship, Genealogical Relatedness and Village Fissioning among the Yanomamo Indians," 491–93, where the author describes a village fissioning process in the 1960s and '70s among the primitive, hunter-gatherer Yanomamo. When a village reached a critical size (100 to 300 people) a group would depart and set up a separate village. It seemed to be invariant that "within-group average relatedness [was] higher in the newly-formed villages than it was in the larger, pre-fission village" (493).

33. "Many have ridiculed the [Westermarck] hypothesis [that incest avoidance occurs naturally as a result of childhood familiarity], imagining that it required some mystical capacity to recognize biological kin. Of course it does not, as Westermarck made clear" (Daly and Wilson, *Sex, Evolution, and Behavior,* 307). See Alexander, *Darwinism and Human Affairs,* 91–92, for a discussion of a genetic base for avoidance of sexual relations with early associates that is augmented by social learning to result in avoidance of sexual relations with close genetic relatives (incest avoidance).
34. A nonbiological explanation for the kibbutzim evidence is noted and countered by van den Berghe, in "Human Inbreeding Avoidance," 102, n. 8, and accompanying text.
35. Demarest, "Does Familiarity Necessarily Lead to Erotic Indifference and Incest Avoidance Because Inbreeding Lowers Reproductive Fitness?" 106–7.
36. See Bermant, "Sexual Behavior: Hard Times with the Coolidge Effect," 76–77: "One day the President and Mrs. Coolidge were visiting a government farm. Soon after their arrival they were taken off on separate tours. When Mrs. Coolidge passed the chicken pens she paused to ask the man in charge if the rooster copulates more than once each day. 'Dozens of times,' was the reply. 'Please tell that to the President,' Mrs. Coolidge requested. When the President passed the pens and was told about the rooster, he asked 'Same hen everytime?' 'Oh no, Mr. President,

a different one each time.' The President nodded slowly, then said, 'Tell that to Mrs. Coolidge.' "

37. Symons, *The Evolution of Human Sexuality*, 208–11.
38. Van den Berghe, "Human Inbreeding Avoidance," 118.
39. Van den Berghe states that his inclination is "to accept the clear evidence for the erotic attraction of novelty, but to believe that the phenomenon is discontinuous when one deals with long-standing, intimate associations in early childhood" (ibid.). By this I take him to mean that a sexual association can become "novel" when a long enough period has elapsed since an earlier association between the same parties.
40. Irons, "Why Lineage Exogamy?" 476, 480; Alexander, *Darwinism and Human Affairs*, 192–93; and van den Berghe, "Human Inbreeding Avoidance," 92.
41. E.g., Okl. Stat. Ann., Title 21, §885 (West 1983): "Persons who, being within the degrees of consanguinity within which marriages are by the laws of the State declared to be incestuous and void, intermarry with each other, or commit adultery or fornication with each other, are punishable by imprisonment in the penitentiary not exceeding ten (10) years."
42. Vernier, *American Family Laws*, 184–87, and Drinan, "The Loving Decision and the Freedom to Marry," 370–71.
43. E.g., Ga. Code., §19-3-3(a)(1982): "Any person who marries a person to whom he knows he is related, either by blood *or by marriage* [emphasis added], as follows:
    (1) Father and daughter or stepdaughter;
    (2) Mother and son or stepson;
    (3) Brother and sister of the whole or the half blood;
    (4) Grandparent and grandchild;
    (5) Aunt and nephew; or
    (6) Uncle and niece
shall be punished by imprisonment for not less than one or more than three years."
44. E.g., Ill. Rev. Stat., Ch. 89, §1 (1966): "[M]arriage between parents and children including grandparents and grandchildren of every degree, between brothers and sisters of the half, as well as the whole blood, between uncles and nieces, aunts and nephews, and between cousins of the first degree are declared to be incestuous and void."

    In Areen, *Cases and Materials on Family Law*, 9, it is reported that "[b]y 1976, all states and the District of Columbia prohibited marriage between parent and child, brother and sister, and aunt and nephew (or uncle and niece). Twenty states and the District of Columbia permitted marriages between first cousins."
45. For the significance of the fractional terms that are used to express genetic relationships see text of chapter I, supra, at note superscript 10.
46. As authority for this statement I can only ask readers whether they are comfortably sure that sanctions against incest would not be applied to them if they unknowingly were to have sexual relations with a close

genetic relative. After answering, read the following authority on the law: "Some statutes [prohibiting incest] expressly require knowledge of the relationship. Where this is not in the statute the accusatory pleading [in the criminal action] need not allege such knowledge but this should not be interpreted to mean that one charged with this offense could not exculpate himself by showing that he did not know, or have reason to know, that the woman was related to him in any degree." (Perkins and Boyce, *Criminal Law*, 461.)

47. Shepher, *Incest: A Biosocial View*, 113–14; Fox, "Kinship Categories as Natural Categories," 132.

48. Breuer, *Sociobiology and the Human Dimension*, 211-12, and Lopreato, *Human Nature and Biocultural Evolution*, 318. See also Fox, "Kinship Categories," 134.

49. Lumsden and Wilson, *Promethean Fire*, 70–71, and Shepher, *Incest: A Biosocial View*, 10–11. See also Lumsden and Wilson, "Translation of Epigenetic Rules of Individual Behavior into Ethnographic Patterns."

50. Shepher, *Incest: A Biosocial View*, 23–24, 179. But see also 113–14.

51. See Shepher, *Incest: A Biosocial View*, 76: "For a prohibition [like the incest taboo] to take root, somebody with power must enforce it and others must comply." And see van den Berghe, "Human Inbreeding Avoidance," 120: "[C]ulture can institutionalize power differentials and favor the fitness of some at the expense of others. . . . Perhaps we should shift from a conventional anthropological notion of culture as a system of shared meanings (with its hidden implications of consensus) to a conception of culture as a set of rules manipulated for gain by actors who often cheat if they can get away with it. . . . Reframed in terms of biological evolution, culture becomes a set of rules that minimizes the cost of playing the social game by smoothing out the rough edges of individual differences, and by creating predictable uniformities."

52. See van den Berghe, "Human Inbreeding Avoidance," particularly his introductory abstract, for use of the term "precultural."

53. See Fox, "Kinship Categories," 134: "[T]he propensity to avoid incest exists; what the taboo does, literally, is to give voice to this propensity via rules couched in language."

54. For use of the term "culturgen" see Lumsden and Wilson, *Promethean Fire*, 121, and Shepher, *Incest: A Biosocial View*, 11.

55. Compare discussion by Alexander of the attachment, by parents in various societies, of the label "incestuous" to whatever marriages they wish to discourage, and his expectation that rulemakers in any society will use the notion of incest avoidance similarly (Alexander, *Darwinism and Human Affairs*, 197).

56. See supra notes 50 and 51. See also Breuer, *Sociobiology and the Human Dimension*, 211: "[T]here is today hardly a human society without incest taboos or laws against incest. In sociobiological perspective this is indeed a paradigmatic case how inborn behavioral tendencies are interpreted by a later cultural superstructure."

57. See supra note 55.
58. In an accidental sample of twenty-two adoptees who had searched for their birth parents, a majority were in their twenties at the inception of the search. The average age of the entire sample at the inception was thirty-one years (Sorosky, Baran, and Pannor, *The Adoption Triangle*, 146-53).
59. Ibid.
60. Laws concerning incest have been enacted in the U.S. by state legislators. It was reported that during the decade ending in 1959, most state legislators were in their late thirties, forties, and fifties (Jewell, *The State Legislature: Politics and Practice*, 32). Although it appears that the average age of state legislators has decreased in recent years (Rosenthal, "The State of State Legislatures: An Overview," 1193), the earlier age picture is probably more representative of the age of those who enacted the legal restrictions concerning incest that are now on the statute books in all fifty states. There is a certain lag time between the onset of any societal attitude that could promote the enactment of a law and the actual enactment of that law.
61. Under certain limited circumstances a close inbreeding route might be the only route by which young individuals could hope to reproduce or at least have the best chance of having their genetic complement well represented in succeeding generations. The calculus of reproductive strategy may make the risk of inbreeding depression a risk worth taking (Shepher, *Incest: A Biosocial View*, 98-104). There has been much discussion of close inbreeding practices reported among royalty in various highly stratified societies as falling in this category (ibid., 130–31).

It is unclear what the calculus of reproductive strategy will indicate for older people in comparatively unstratified societies like the U.S. who have all or the bulk of their personal child-generating years behind them, but it is worth noting that their continuing genetic reproductive interests will tend to lie principally with a broad base of younger relatives with whom they have considerable genetic overlap. Cf. Kurland, "Paternity, Mother's Brother, and Human Sociality," 171.
62. Oakley made an observation that would have caught anyone's eye. Before relating it, let me provide some background.

Biologists have observed that human females have more at stake, in genetic reproductive calculus terms, than do males in any given reproductive effort. From these facts sociobiologists predict that evolutionary processes should have inclined females to be more resistant to incest than males because incest is a high-risk reproductive strategy (Shepher, *Incest: A Biosocial View*, 128–29; van den Berghe, "Human Inbreeding Avoidance," 98). Empirical evidence has shown that females are more resistant (ibid).

Oakley noted a study showing that an overwhelming majority of a group of fifty adoptees who searched for their birth parents were females (Oakley, "Sociobiology and the Law," at 50). That information might suggest that such searches have genetic programming behind them in view of the biological tenet that females generally have more reason than males to avoid incest. But two things detract from the Oakley observation. The first is that any discrepancy between females and males regarding searching activity could be due to relatively "pure" culturization. One professional observer believes that "one reason so few men are searching is that boys are encouraged by society to deny hurt feelings" (Lifton, "The Search," *New York Times Magazine*, Jan. 25, 1975, 15, 20). Secondly, the survey cited by Oakley was admitted by the researchers themselves to be methodologically flawed (Baran, Sorosky, and Pannor, "The Dilemma of Our Adoptees," 38; Sorosky, Baran, and Pannor, "The Effects of the Sealed Record in Adoption," 900, 901) and has been countered, since Oakley's observation, by a study based on a larger sample, which showed only some "slight evidence" that females were more active in seeking information about birth parents. The researchers in the later study applied various measurements of such activity (Feigelman and Silverman, *Chosen Children*, 217).

63. For theory as to when circumstances calling for "mutuality" (cooperation) lead to kin grouping together, see Wrangham, "Mutualism, Kinship and Social Evolution."

64. See van den Berghe, "Human Inbreeding Avoidance," 93: "Given the benefits of kin selection or nepotism in the maximization of inclusive fitness [citing authorities], social animals draw benefits by living among kin." But see Dawkins, "Opportunity Costs of Inbreeding," 106: "Remember . . . that surrounding yourself with relatives cuts both ways: Near neighbors may, indeed, be well placed to exchange favors with you, but they are also your closest and severest competitors for the necessities of life."

65. Alexander, "The Evolution of Social Behavior," 356.

66. See Alcock, *Animal Behavior*, 520.

67. Sociobiologists suggest that our core behavioral tendencies developed over five million years and have changed very little in the last ten thousand years (E. O. Wilson, *On Human Nature*, 34; Barash, *Sociobiology and Behavior*, 311). However, gene/culture coevolutionary equations have been employed to suggest that "substantial genetic evolution can occur in the epigenetic rules guiding thought and behavior" in as little as one thousand years (Lumsden and Wilson, *Promethean Fire*, 152). In the critique of sociobiology, *Vaulting Ambition* (1985), by P. Kitcher, the author, while not denying the thousand-year rule, suggests reasons why it would apply only to "people of extraordinary stupidity" (390).

68. See supra note 32.

69. See supra note 33 and accompanying text.

70. See Boorman and Levitt, *The Genetics of Altruism*, 16: "In kin selection, cooperation among organisms bearing 'altruistic' genes is based on recognition of kin. Such 'recognition' need involve no elaborate mechanisms. For example, in a species with low powers of dispersal 'kin-

altruist' behavior may simply be behavior directed toward *all* fellow species members with whom a given individual has associated since birth [citing authorities]."
And *cf.* Fox, "Kinship Categories," 137.

71. See supra the text between note superscripts 24 and 33.
72. Dawkins, *The Selfish Gene*, 32–34.
73. See generally Beckstrom, *Sociobiology and the Law*.

Chapter
VI

Avoiding and Reforming Laws Resulting from Unconscious Self-Serving Lawmaking

It is an ideal of democratic societies that lawmakers promulgate rules and decide cases in an impartial, objective, truthseeking manner. In most discussions of the use of biocultural science in the legal process, it is convenient and harmless to assume that the ideal reflects reality—that subjectivity does not creep into lawmakers' actions. Thus when U.S. lawmakers announce that they are seeking to distribute the property of people who die without a will in the way that those people typically would want it done, one can say, "That's your goal? Well then, here is a group of scientists you should meet who might help you achieve it." Someone might suggest that lawmakers would really prefer to keep a free hand, unencumbered by scientific learning on the matter, because by so doing they could mold the law to serve their own interests in the distribution of decedents' estates. I would answer that uncharitable suggestion by observing that the public interest in such cases is, nevertheless, well served by taking the lawmakers at their word when they say they are aiming for objective standards, and by introducing them to scientists who might assist them in reaching those goals. But in this chapter I want to look directly at the possibility of subjectivity in lawmaking and point out that sociobiology suggests there may be a kind of subjectivity operating in lawmakers of which even they are not aware.

Most people will find it easy to accept the idea that lawmakers sometimes are motivated by self-interest when they promulgate rules that are applicable to the entire population. Enough is known about blatant self-serving rulemaking by autocrats and monarchs in human history to give rise to suspicion that there has been considerable disguised activity of a similar kind even in representative democracies. If Henry VIII was prompted, as he was, to manipulate the rules regarding dissolution of marriage and succession of offspring to the throne to serve his reproductive interests,[1] there is reason to suspect that bodies of legislators or judges have occasionally acted in their self-interest when the rule being announced was arguably in the interests of the population in general.

Henry VIII was undoubtedly well aware that the laws he prompted were to his advantage, and when one contemplates similar action by legislators or judges, one normally would have in mind situations where the lawmakers were consciously aware that the action served them well personally. It may be less easy for the layperson to accept the following concept: evolutionary processes may have resulted in people in lawmaking positions acting on occasion in their own self-interest without consciously recognizing the fact. I find that concept to be one of the most intriguing potential applications of sociobiological theory to the lawmaking process.

Let me, at this point, ask the reader whether the following legal actions by United States lawmakers appear to have been in the self-interest of the majority of those who promulgated them:

1. Federal legislation in the 1970s and '80s that raised, from $60,000 to $600,000, the value of a decedent's estate that is exempt from taxation.
2. A 1918 U.S. Supreme Court decision that declared that federal legislation restricting the employment of young children in factories was unconstitutional.

I suspect the reader will more readily perceive self-interest in the first example than in the second. But even in the first example, a detailed analysis may reveal more than is initially apparent. I will eventually detail, in these and similar examples, how self-interest of the lawmakers may be lurking in various obscure degrees. I use the term self-interest here in a broad sociobiological sense upon which I will presently elaborate.

But if self-interest, however defined, is present in these actions by lawmakers, evolutionary biologists suggest that the responsible lawmakers themselves may have been less able than objective observers to detect it. Thus if the self-interest seems obscure to you and me, the theory suggests that it might have been even more obscure to the responsible lawmakers involved because of evolved self-deception. If the theory should prove to be correct in this particular, the insights it provides eventually could be of value to the lawmaking process. Before elaborating on that point, let me review and outline the relevant theory regarding the concepts of "self"-interest and evolved self-deception.

"Self"-Interested Conduct

One does not need sociobiological theory to establish the core component of what I will define as self-interest in this chapter. When I act to obtain food, clothing, shelter, educational opportunities, leisure time, etc., for the being within my skin, that is action in my self-interest and my use of those things is of personal benefit to me. If science should add the explanation that such behavior has the ultimate objective of putting me in a position optimally to reproduce my genetic material and to nurture others in whom it is contained, the explanation would put a gloss on this popular core concept of self-interested behavior, but not really expand it. Furthermore, many laypeople may readily accept the idea that when a person acts to benefit a relative, such as a child or a nephew, there is actually a benefit to the actor as well. The popular concept of nepotism usually means that a relative has been given a job at least partly because of the relationship and not strictly on merit. But, beyond that, is it not true that we perceive the employer's *motivation* for bestowing this benefit on the employee/relative as being something close to selfishness?

Sociobiologists have adopted the word nepotism and given it an expanded and slightly altered definition: to them it encompasses behavior of an individual that benefits a person or persons with whom that individual has a high degree of genetic overlap.[2] And when an individual does benefit such close relatives, sociobiological theory provides an explanation for any impression the layperson may have that the behavior is somehow "selfish."

We can start with the now generally accepted proposition that in natural selection what has been selected or differentially proliferated, for the most part at least,[3] is genes—or, more precisely, combinations of genetic materials. The gene combinations affecting behavior that have been most successful in the proliferation process and thus are well represented in organisms living today are those that have well-programmed their carriers—such as human beings—to behave in ways that promote the genes' proliferation.

Here again comes the tricky part—the working concept of evolutionary biology that may be the most difficult to grasp: when two or more organisms, such as two humans, contain the same gene, those separate manifestations may be conceptualized as identical copies of the same thing. All copies of a gene can be thought of as collectively making up a single entity, and each of them are of equal value to the entity. Therefore, the genes or gene combinations affecting behavior that have been most successful from generation to generation in the evolutionary process (and thus are well represented in today's collective human gene pool) are those that have programmed a human carrier in ways that promote not only the survival of, and reproduction by, that person, but also the survival of, and reproduction by, other people who carry high percentages of the same genetic material.

From this viewpoint one can look upon genes or gene combinations as being the "self" when one searches for "self-interest" in the activities of their human carriers. And the "self" exists not only in any individual person in focus, but in his or her close genetic relatives as well, to various lesser degrees.

The concept of genetic self-interest extends further. Inasmuch as an individual needs someone of the opposite sex for the purposes of reproducing and helping to nurture offspring, sociobiologists suggest that our biological programming inclines us to be virtually as solicitous of the welfare of our spouses and our "blood" (close genetic) relatives' mates as we are of the welfare of the blood relatives themselves.[4] Thus sociobiological theory endorses any impression a layperson may have that something selfish is going on when an elected official secures a government appointment for his or her son-in-law. So sociobiology provides a possible articulated explanation for any intuitive popular feeling that assisting relatives, whether by blood or marriage, is selfish conduct.

But the sociobiological concept of "self"-interested conduct extends even further. It can extend to a favor done for a nonrelative. At this point the correspondence of the sociobiological concept to popular intuitive perceptions is quite vague, but with a little explanation the layperson should accept that even a favor done for a nonrelative can ultimately prove to be "selfish." Virtually all adults have had occasion to realize that a favor done today for a friend or associate can produce a future return benefit for themselves or for their close relatives. And frequently, if not always, such actors have the hope or expectation that the return benefit will be more valuable to them than what they have given up. When a favor is done under such circumstances, the layperson should accept that the act is not purely unselfish.

Favors done under such circumstances illustrate the sociobiologists' reciprocal "altruism" concept.[5] That concept in its full development suggests that true altruism seldom, if ever, occurs. Even a favor done for a stranger with whom the actor is not likely to have any other association is said to be almost always, if not always, motivated, consciously or unconsciously, by an expected return from some quarter for the actor's genetic complement.[6]

Indeed, from an evolutionary biological viewpoint one might characterize *any* official conduct by public officials as selfishly motivated, if for no other reason than that they are doing it in order to retain their jobs, or at least to gain the general esteem of the community for themselves and their families, which could eventually redound to the benefit of their genetic complement. From this unlimited perspective, "self-interested" conduct could include discretionary acts that cause *immediate*, direct damage or loss to officials and their social circles, as well as purely ministerial, nondiscretionary acts in view of the fact that an *eventual* indirect gain from such acts is likely. But, of course, the general public does not frown on such acts or the indirect benefits they may eventually return to officials. So, for the purpose of critiquing the performance of public servant lawmakers, we will exclude such approved conduct from our working definition of self-interested official conduct. Let us include only discretionary official conduct likely to result in benefits to lawmakers themselves and/or their close relatives, friends, and associates as a result of *relatively direct* operative effects of the conduct, which benefits are likely to be disproportionately large compared to that received by the average citizen (and/or the citizen's close relatives, friends, and associates) affected by the conduct.

Evolved Self-Deception

Sociobiologists have been disturbed by the initial negative reception that sociobiological concepts often—or perhaps usually—receive from intelligent laypeople.[7] Even some prominent sociobiologists will admit to having at least been perplexed by the idea that we can generally be expected to behave toward others in such a way as to maximize the reproduction of the genetic material that we contain.[8] This consternation is probably not surprising when one realizes that a refinement of the idea results in the suggestion that virtually all of our behavior can be called "selfish," for lack of a better word. Who among us likes to think of ourselves in that light? But emotional negative reaction to the theory has occurred even when writers have employed the arguably justifiable device of somewhat relieving us of personal responsibility by blaming such predispositions, metaphorically, on programming by our "selfish genes."[9]

It appears possible that a large part of the difficulty we have in accepting the idea that we are selfishly motivated may be due to the selective process of evolution. Sociobiologists have suggested that the genetic material affecting the relevant behavior of those people whose selfish motivations were successfully concealed from others has historically been more successful in the genetic reproductive process than the similar genetic material contained in people whose selfish motivations were easily detected.[10] Perhaps the best insurance against revealing self-interest during conduct is for actors themselves to be unaware of their self-interest so that their demeanor does not "give the game away." Therefore, theorists have assumed that, at least in many areas of the social arena, "we have evolved to deceive even ourselves about our true motives."[11] Thus the theory suggests we are sometimes unaware that what we are doing is in our self-interest, while it may be apparent to other people observing our conduct.[12]

We should note that sociobiologists are not talking here about the confidence-building bravado we sometimes call self-deception, as in "that little man is fooling himself if he thinks he can lift that boulder." Instead, the theorists are referring to an inter- *and* intrapersonal deception on a deception, as in "that fellow is trying to pull the wool over our eyes, and *he doesn't even realize it himself.*"

This concept has not been fully developed by theorists. In particular, it is not clear when this self-deception mechanism ought to be expected to operate. Clearly it is not always operative. You and I are often well aware that we are acting in our self-interest, and we find it difficult, if not impossible, to conceal the fact that we are aware of it. When we are caught with our hands in a cookie jar, our fluster and blushing are hard to suppress. On the other hand, let us picture a mother, father, and their child in the family kitchen. It is fairly easy to accept that the father would not immediately recognize his self-interest when, as mother opens the cookie jar to help herself, he explains to the observing youngster that mothers occasionally need the sugar in cookies in order to create quickly the necessary energy to do their household chores (and you also, father?) for the benefit of the whole family. It is hard to describe the difference between this last scenario where the self-deception mechanism may well be operative and the simple "caught in the cookie jar" case where it is not. I will leave it to scientists eventually to tell us where the self-deception mechanism is likely to operate.[13] I am satisfied that my readers and I can think of examples where the mechanism might be operative, and that is sufficient for the purposes of this chapter.

Those purposes are two: First, I want to suggest that general awareness of the sociobiological self-deception concept, after it has been well developed and substantiated, could encourage objective observers to look for and point out instances where lawmakers might be unwittingly making rules in their own self-interest. Second, I want to suggest that if lawmakers became aware that self-deception concerning self-interested conduct, as well as the conduct itself, may be products of evolutionary processes, they might more easily accept critiques by objective observers and that could facilitate law reform.[14]

Potential Benefits of Evolutionary Learning to the Law Reform Process

In a representative democracy, if a rule is promulgated that disproportionately benefits a narrow group that includes the lawmakers, it need not necessarily be objectionable to other elements in the population. But it might be. If it is, lawmakers as well as other elements of the population could benefit from perceiving the disproportionate gain to the lawmakers. The realization value to those outside the in-group is obvious. But lawmakers in the in-group could also benefit—through avoiding embarrassment or something worse, like job loss—by abandoning or altering a self-serving rule before it is promulgated, or by eliminating or altering one already in effect before the nature of the rule is discovered and pointed out by other elements of the population.

Even if obscure self-interest of the lawmakers were first detected and alleged by others, avoidance or reform of the law might be facilitated if lawmakers generally became aware of sociobiology. It seems safe to observe that we humans tend to be more willing to admit that we are acting in our self-interest when we can deflect the blame for so doing. I have been impressed by sociobiology's potential value in this regard for those who would like to see humans act in a more selfless manner.

Sociobiologists are quick to point out that individual willpower and collective action can overcome selfish predispositions.[15] Thus, ultimately, the theorists rob us of any excuse for giving in to the predispositions. Nevertheless, one can rationally blame the initial selfish impulses on evolutionary processes if sociobiologists are right. If lawmakers became aware of this, the law reform process could be facilitated: when someone pointed out to them that they acted, in a relatively obscure and possibly unconscious manner, in their self-interest, they should find it easier to accept the fact and take corrective action.[16] Blame for their prior conduct could be deflected to programming by their "selfish genes."[17]

Of course, even with a knowledge of sociobiology, in a given case the reactions of lawmakers when the self-serving aspect of the law or ruling is uncovered might not be avoidance or reform, but a search for unselfish public rationalizations in order to save the legal measure. So be it. In respect to legislation and court-made rules (in a system where judges are elected), as long as society has a well-enfranchised electoral system and a free press, the public rationale had best be a good one. In any case, I for one am a firm believer in the virtue of full illumination of the field upon which the game is played, so that the group with the ball, as well as the opposition and spectators, can see what the group is doing.

Some self-serving lawmaking is so obviously in the interests of the lawmakers as to need no illumination from science or elsewhere. When Congress votes itself a pay raise, the only points for debate are whether rationales such as the public need for competent representation and current relatively high salaries in the private sector outweigh the obvious self-interest of the act. I will eventually elaborate on other examples wherein a possible benefit to the lawmakers is to me less evident. But first let me set out some guidelines which may assist those looking for lawmakers' "self"-interest, defined in the expanded sense I earlier described. They are guidelines which may or may not have intuitively occurred to me before I began reading sociobiological writings.

Distinguishing Characteristics of Lawmakers

In a representative lawmaking body, self-interested rulemaking by members tends to be discouraged when members of interest groups in the society are represented by members of the lawmaking body in roughly corresponding numbers. On the other hand, when the lawmakers are predominantly members of only a limited number of the many competing interest groups in society, self-interested rulemaking by the lawmakers is more likely. Thus when we prepare to look for self-interest of lawmakers in their official actions, we should seek to identify characteristics of lawmakers that have tended to distinguish them, as a group, from other elements of the population.

From my thirty years of observing the legal system I have the distinct impression that American lawmakers have tended historically, and to date, clearly to be:

1. in possession of above-average financial means,
2. more closely related to, and engaged in reciprocal associations with, people who have high educational attainments and above-

average financial means than is the average member of the population,

3. male, and
4. middle-aged or older.

These characteristics are not necessarily listed in order of prominence, nor is the list exhaustive. I am reasonably confident, though, that my suggestions would be borne out by empirical research. Information presently available is supportive.[18] All four items on this list figure prominently in my examples, which we will now examine, of legal actions where the possible self-interest of the lawmakers was not immediately obvious to me.

Some of these examples may yet have escaped my notice had I not been sensitized by exposure to the details of sociobiological theory concerning our predispositions to act not only in our own interests, but also in the interests of close relatives and of close friends and associates with whom we have developed reciprocal aid-giving relationships. The theory suggests that, to the extent such "self"-interest is not immediately obvious to you and me, it would have been even less obvious to the responsible lawmakers whose interests were well served.

Finding "Self"-Interest

In the following illustrative analyses of legal actions by United States lawmakers, I do not mean to imply that the actions were wrong *in any sense*, such as having the wrong effects on society or benefiting the wrong elements in society. Also, I do not mean to suggest that any of the legal actions illustrated were wrong in the sense that any actual or potential benefits to the lawmakers or their genetic complements were benefits to which the lawmakers were not "entitled," in some grand reckoning, as a type of compensation for sacrifices made as public servants. Such judgments are value-laden, and I wish to avoid them.

Similarly, in terms of balance sheet accounting, I will not attempt to subtract credits from debits. Thus if a body should give something away and thereby deprive itself, and then later take that same thing back, I will view the last act in isolation and treat it as being self-interested for purposes of this exercise.

In searching for self-interest in the conduct of lawmakers, I will look only for *benefits* that could flow from the legal action. I am aware that when one person or group benefits more than others from an action, the corresponding costs to the others are not necessarily just the negative image of the difference in benefits. The calculation of costs and benefits depends, to a large extent, on how those terms are defined and measured. If I take the last bit of food that is available to us, say, an apple, I may benefit from my action more than you do, but the cost to your vitality is less if you are well fed than if you are starving. In this exercise I will not attempt to assess the ultimate costs to others of the lawmakers' actions. I will be satisfied if I can show how it could have been anticipated at the time of the actions that the lawmakers would get more apples than most other citizens and thereby "benefit" more. If they were likely to benefit more, I will say that the action was in their self-interest.

Finally, I do not pretend that I have uncovered all the factors that might make the legal actions more or less "self"-interested in terms of exhaustive sociobiological calculations. My aims are more modest. I want only to illustrate how one might approach an isolated legal action from a sociobiological viewpoint in an effort to uncover the self-interest of the responsible lawmakers in the particular legal action in focus.

With this limited goal in mind, let us approach the following prominent instances of legal conduct in the U.S. during the twentieth century by applying the test for self-interest that I mentioned earlier. The question is: *Was the discretionary legal action likely to result in benefits to a majority of the responsible lawmakers (and/or their close relatives, friends, and associates) as a result of relatively direct operative effects of the action, which benefits would be disproportionately large compared to that received by the average citizen (and/or the citizen's close relatives, friends, and associates) affected by the action?* (Hereafter, when I refer to "friends," it will be meant to include associates, such as employers, with whom the person may or may not be "friendly.")

1. *Federal legislation in the 1970s and '80s that raised, from $60,000 to $600,000, the value of a decedent's estate that is exempt from taxation.*[19]

Most of the legislators had, and/or could have expected to have at the time of their death, property worth more than $60,000, so they would benefit from the change in the law.[20] Their close friends and relatives, including those from whom they were likely to inherit property, would also have tended to be in those financial circumstances. On the other hand, the majority of the population would fall below the $60,000 figure and thus would not benefit from the change in the law.[21] Furthermore, it seems likely that the majority of the legislators would not fall above the $600,000 figure.[22] Therefore, the upward adjustment of the exemption would appear to stop at about the point where it would cease to benefit the majority of the responsible lawmakers.

2. *State supreme court rulings that in a dissolving family where there*

is a legal dispute as to custody of young children, there shall be no pre-sumption in favor of mothers; the gender of the contending parent shall not be a consideration.[23]

By eliminating the prior rule favoring mothers and thus neutralizing the gender factor, the legal actions benefited fathers. The courts involved were predominantly, if not exclusively, composed of males. It is probable that while only a portion of the middle-aged or older male judges were fathers of minor children at the time of these rulings, in most cases there remained the biological possibility that they might be in the future.[24] And, needless to say, those male judges would never be mothers of young children.

Genetic relatives of the judges, as well as the judges' friends, were also potential competitors in child custody disputes. Collectively, the judges should have had roughly as many relatives and friends who were female as were male. However, the fact that the male judges had, and/or could have, minor children more closely related to themselves (one-half genetic relationship)[25] than the minor offspring of any of those relatives or friends should clearly offset the balance and lead sociobiologists to predict a collective bias of the lawmakers toward fathers.

3. *Federal government decisions in the early 1970s that terminated the drafting of young men into the armed services and thereby established all-voluntary armed services.*

After the Second World War, Congress periodically authorized the executive branch, for specified periods, to induct young men into the armed services. When the last such authorization ended in 1973, it was not renewed. Indeed, the executive branch ceased exercising its powers to draft before the last authorization period expired.[26]

It was thus not action, but inaction by Congress and the executive branch that brought about termination of the draft. Relatively little responsibility can be put upon the general membership of Congress for failure to address an issue that is never presented to it in the form of a bill or resolution. In this case it appears that responsibility for the decision *not* to continue the draft rests not so much with Congress as a whole as with certain prime movers in Congress, as well as members of President Nixon's administration.[27] Together these people may be considered as the lawmakers responsible for the elimination of the draft.

Surely few, if any, of the responsible lawmakers were young enough to have been caught up in the draft system, but they had children, grandchildren, and other close relatives and friends who were eligible. Furthermore, those relatives and friends would have tended to be formally educated and financially endowed to the extent that voluntary entry into the armed services, with its attendant dangers, would have held less attraction for them than for the average young person in the U.S. population. And to the extent that those relatives and friends would be relieved of the burden of having to spend time in the role of a draftee, they would be free to devote that time to the pursuit of relatively more remunerative and prestigious occupations, which their backgrounds had better prepared them for than that of the average young person.

4. *A 1918 U.S. Supreme Court decision which declared that federal legislation restricting the employment of young children in factories was unconstitutional.*[28]

An anticipated result of the Court's action was that existing child labor practices would continue. Child labor was cheap labor,[29] which meant that the Court's ruling could have translated into financial savings for various elements of the population. These savings could have been passed on to consumers of the employers' products. The Supreme Court justices were consumers, but they were probably indistinguishable from the rest of population in that regard, so no disproportionate gain to them was likely on that count.

Consumer interests aside, the employers affected were most likely to benefit from the continuing use of child labor.[30] Those employers tended to be wealthy and powerful people—the sort with whom the justices were likely to have close reciprocal associations. So, the justices' self-interest, in its broad sociobiological sense, might appear to have been served by their action overturning the legislation restricting child labor. But, could they also have benefited from upholding it?

The immediate beneficiaries of the legislation restricting child labor, which the Court struck down, were intended to be the children who might otherwise be employed. It is arguable that the whole of society, including the justices, their relatives, and friends, would ultimately benefit from the legislation in that a healthier young America would be a result.[31] But, to the extent that there would have been a more immediate, larger benefit to the social group comprised of the affected children themselves and their circles of relatives and friends, the justices and their circles would have tended to be outside of it. The social group surrounding the justices would have generally had the financial means to keep their young children from laboring in factories in any event.

Conclusion

Have I analyzed these five situations correctly in my attempt to detect the broadly defined self-interest of the lawmakers? Perhaps not. The exercise was meant only to illustrate the way in which a knowledge of sociobiology, if and when its precepts become well substantiated, might better equip observers to examine a piece of lawmaking with a view toward detecting the self-interest of the lawmakers—self-interest obscure enough that the lawmakers themselves may not have been aware, due to biologically evolved self-deception, that their actions were promoting it.

The suspicion that people who are put in positions of public trust often act in their self-interest without detection is not a new idea. And the intuitive feeling that when actors aid members of their families they are doing something essentially selfish has probably been around for a long time also. The concept that when actors aid friends or associates, they may be acting selfishly is less firmly fixed as a matter of public intuition, but it vaguely appears to exist as well. Sociobiological theory holds the potential to scientifically illuminate and define these intuitive feelings and help us to better appraise whether lawmakers are serving their total constituencies.

To the extent that public awareness of sociobiology ultimately provides means with which to expose the relatively obscure self-interest of lawmakers, it may be thought of as giving ammunition to critics of any existing lawmaking establishment. What I have suggested in this chapter should have equal relevance and utility whatever the political complexion of a society, as long as that society has entities within it that function as lawmakers for the society as a whole. If sociobiology does eventually serve reform purposes in this nonpartisan manner, it will prove interesting—in view of the widespread initial reaction to sociobiology which focused only on its possible misuse in justifying conservative positions.[32]

The most valuable contribution of sociobiology to a campaign to avoid self-serving lawmaking and reform self-serving laws could be the insight that people may be programmed by the processes of evolution to have a blind spot when it comes to recognizing obscure self-interest in activities that they themselves undertake. If this is true and lawmakers became aware of this fact, they might more easily accept criticism of their actions and more readily take corrective measures.

At this point, we should recall the sociobiological position on the free will of the individual that we explored in chapter III.[33] If completely unselfish behavior—"true" altruism—is more than can be expected, even from lawmakers acting in their official capacities, something less might nevertheless be promoted through a knowledge of human natural history. Many more lawmakers might be persuaded to do what many presumably have already done: postpone a return to their genetic complement by making laws that are best for their total constituencies with the expectation that the resulting good public reputation will keep them in office and otherwise redound, in indirect ways, to their benefit and the benefit of their present and future close relatives.

NOTES

1. Henry VIII's attempts to produce an heir by marrying a succession of women was temporarily thwarted by the pope. Subsequently parliament enacted a series of laws that ended papal jurisdiction in England, initially declared certain female children as successors, and finally set the stage for the succession of Edward VII. See generally Parmiter, *The King's Great Matter: A Study of Anglo-Papal Relations, 1527–1534.* "Since Henry and the country at large were of an anti-clerical cast of mind, their identity of interest produced an harmony of opinion . . . and Henry was sufficiently skillful to make use of this harmony to manipulate both houses of parliament" (116).
2. See Alexander, "The Evolution of Social Behavior," 356. See also Hamilton, "The Evolution of Altruistic Behavior," and "The Genetical Evolution of Social Behavior," I & II, 16.
3. On the theory concerning the relative importance of selection at the level of groups of individuals as opposed to the level of the genes or genetic material that individuals contain, see Williams, *Adaptation and Natural Selection,* 92–250; Williams, ed., *Group Selection;* Barash, *Sociobiology and Behavior,* 107–15, 125–28; and Brandon and Burian, eds., *Genes, Organisms, Populations: Controversies Over the Units of Selection.*
4. See Irons, "Human Female Reproductive Strategies," 169, 200–203, and Alexander, *Darwinism and Human Affairs,* 159–60. See also Flinn, "Resources, Mating, and Kinship: The Behavioral Ecology of a Trinidadian Village," 44: "[Aid-giving inclinations] among those linked by a mating relationship . . . are dependent upon the probability that the mating relationship will be maintained."
5. See Trivers, "The Evolution of Reciprocal Altruism," 189.
6. See Alexander, *The Biology of Moral Systems,* 82, 94, 97.
7. See generally various essays in Montagu, ed., *Sociobiology Examined,* which are not, however, strictly lay reactions since, for some of the authors, sociobiology could be seen as a threat to their established professional positions.
8. Cf. Dawkins, *The Blind Watchmaker,* 3: "I myself flatly refused to believe Darwin's theory when I first heard about it as a child."
9. See the reaction of Midgley to Dawkins's metaphorical approach in *The*

Selfish Gene (1976) in *Gene Juggling* (1979), reprinted in Montagu, ed., *Sociobiology Examined*, 108.

10. Alexander, *Darwinism and Human Affairs*, 134–39; Alexander, "The Search for a General Theory of Behavior," 96–97; and Trivers, *Social Evolution*, 415–20. See Ruse, *Sociobiology: Sense or Nonsense*, 204–5, 69.

11. Alexander, *Darwinism and Human Affairs*, 134. See also Alexander, *The Biology of Moral Systems*, 123: "Self-deception . . . may not be a pathological or detrimental trait, at least in most people most of the time. Rather it may have evolved as a way to deceive *others*. Self-deception is unlike at least *some* deception of others in that it need have no conscious aspect: the self-deceiver does not (necessarily) know he is deceiving himself. The *direct* other-deceiver usually (at least) does."

12. "We know that different people have different evolutionary interests. We know, from sociobiology, that people will 'see' that which is in their evolutionary interests to see" (Ruse, *Sociobiology: Sense or Nonsense*, 204).

13. Alexander explores the possibility that the mechanism operates in regard to human ovulation because "[t]he human female clearly has not evolved to keep knowledge of ovulation in the center of her consciousness, where, in view of its importance, we might expect it to be" (Alexander, *Darwinism and Human Affairs*, 135). See also Alexander, *The Biology of Moral Systems*, 153.

14. See Trivers, "The Evolution of Reciprocal Altruism," 416: "Of course it must be advantageous for the truth to be registered somewhere, so that the mechanisms of self-deception are expected to reside side-by-side with mechanisms for the correct apprehension of reality. The mind must be structured in a very complex fashion, repeatedly split into public and private portions, with complicated interactions between the subsections." Trivers describes a study by Gur and Sackeim involving voice recognition which demonstrated in that context that (1) true and false information is simultaneously stored in a single person, (2) the false information is stored in the conscious mind, and the true information is unconscious, and (3) self-deception is motivated with reference to others (ibid., 416–18).

    See also Lockard, "Speculations on the Adaptive Significance of Self-Deception," 257, where the author summarizes research on proximal neurophysiological mechanisms that could be instrumental in the self-deception process.

15. See, e.g., Alexander, "Natural Selection and Societal Laws," 249, 277–78.

16. See supra note 12. See also Alexander, *Darwinism and Human Affairs*, 135–36: "Eventually we ought to be able to disentangle and make sense of an enormous number of social interactions with particular historical significance within the context of self-deception. I assume that such insights will help free us from insecurities, uneasiness, and sources of tension and unhappiness which are all too often cryptic and unconscious. I assume that such insights will disencumber our efforts to pursue social interactions disinterestedly."

17. See Alexander, *The Biology of Moral Systems*, 120–21: "Conscious con-

cealment of interests, or disavowal, is deliberate deception, considered more reprehensible than anything not conscious. Indeed, if one does not know consciously what his interests are, he cannot, in *some* sense, be accused of deception even though he may be using an evolved ability of self-deception to deceive others."

18. In order to provide a comparison to the information provided below of characteristics of recent U.S. lawmakers, it will be useful to have the information concerning characteristics of the U.S. population in general provided in tables 1-3 at the bottom of this page.

Federal Legislators. The base salary of senators and representatives in 1981 was $60,662.50 (*Congressional Quarterly Almanac*, 399–400).

In the 98th Congress (1983–85), 61 of 100 senators and 200 of 435 representatives held law degrees (*Congressional Quarterly Almanac*, 29).

There were 13 women in Congress during the 1963–65 session, and 21 during the 1981–83 session (*Congress and the Nation*, 12-13, 27).

From 1963 to 1983 the average age of members of Congress ranged from 53.0 to 49.2 years (ibid.).

By using various objective criteria, one author concluded that U.S. senators holding office between 1947 and 1950 had "relatively high class origins" (Matthews, *U.S. Senators and Their World*, 17-21, 27)

Federal Judges. A sampling of district court judges in the first, second, third, and fourth circuits in the late 1970s showed an average age of 58.5 years.

Regarding colleges or universities attended, the breakdown was: Ivy league school, 32 percent; private school, 40.2 percent; public school, 18.2 percent; information not available or did not attend, 9.8 percent

Table 1.

Year	Median Age of Population
1960	29.5
1970	28.1
1980	30.0

Sources: Bureau of Census, U.S. Department of Commerce, *Historical Statistics of the United States, Colonial Times to 1970*, 19; and the Bureau of the Census, U.S. Dept. of Commerce, *Statistical Abstract of the United States: 1986*, 25.

Table 2.

Year	Median Household Income
1981	$19,074
1984	$22,415

Source: *Statistical Abstract*, 447.

Table 3.

Year	Percentage of Population over Age 25 Who Have Completed at Least One Year of College
1980	31.9
1984	34.9

Source: *Statistical Abrstract*, 133.

(Kitchen, *Federal District Judges: An Analysis of Judicial Perceptions*, 161–65).

State Legislators. Jewell (*The State Legislature: Politics and Practice*, 32) reported that during the decade beginning in 1949, most state legislators were "in their late thirties, forties, and fifties. The overwhelming majority of them [were] men, although most legislatures [had] a few women in them. Their education level [was] high, far above the average for their states. About three quarters of them [had] attended college, roughly half of them [had] graduated from college, and a substantial portion [had] attended law school or some other professional or graduate school. Most legislators [had] middle-class or upper-class family backgrounds; their fathers [were] likely to have been engaged in professional or business occupations or at least in such skilled work as farming. . . ."

In the early 1980s Rosenthal reported that state legislators were 97 percent male and, on the average, were in their late thirties. Seventy-five percent possessed at least a bachelor's degree ("The State of State Legislatures: An Overview," 1185, 1193).

State Judges. As of December 31, 1985, the average salary of judges in the highest courts in the fifty states was $66,974; in intermediate appellate courts it was $66,639; in general trial courts, $60,064 (*Legal Times*, Mar. 24, 1986, p. 2, cols. 1, 2, 3).

In a survey of some three thousand judges serving in trial courts of general jurisdiction in the states and the District of Columbia during 1977, they were found to be 98 percent male and to have an average age of 53.4 years (Ryan, Ashman, Sales, and Shane-Dubow, *American Trial Judges*, 128).

19. In addition to the amount in question, which has been termed an "exemption," subtractions can also be made from the gross estate due to "deductions," for example, for gifts to charities.

The issue of what dollar value of a decedent's property is exempt from federal taxation has been complicated by the tendency of statutes and regulations to lump lifetime gifts together with postmortem dispositions. But, assuming that no large gifts are made during one's lifetime, by enactments of the 94th and 96th Congresses, a credit equivalent to a $600,000 exemption took effect in 1987. See 26 U.S.C. §2010 (1982). This U.S. Code provision was added by Pub. L. 94-455, Title XX, §2001(a)(2), Oct. 4, 1976, 90 Stat. 1848, and amended by Pub. L. 97-34, Title IV, §401(a)(1), (2)(A), Aug. 13, 1981, 95 Stat. 299. The exemption prior to 1977 was $60,000. See Act of Aug. 16, 1954, Ch. 736, 68A Stat. 389 (repealed 1976).

20. In 1981 it was reported that 17 senators and 24 representatives had assets of over $1 million. Eleven more senators and 43 more representatives had assets of over $500,000. "Such figures reflect just the tip of the iceberg as far as congressional wealth is concerned. The Ethics in Government Act permits lawmakers to list their assets, liabilities and outside income in extremely broad categories that may lead to substantial

understatement of their net worth" ("Lawmakers' Latest Report on Their Wealth," *U.S. News and World Rep.*, June 1, 1981, 25).

21. "As a result of the unified credit [Tax Reform Act of 1976], less than 2 percent of decedents dying each year will be subject to estate tax, compared to 7 percent under the prior $60,000 exemption" (Surrey, Warren, McDaniel, and Gutman, *Federal Wealth Transfer Taxation*, 829).

22. See supra note 18.

23. Some of these rulings were based on judicially determined policy grounds with no reference to statutory support, such as *In re Marriage of Bowe*, 219 N.W.2d 683 (Iowa 1974), and *Lane v. Lane*, 446 A.2d 418 (Me. 1982). Others relied on statutes which did not directly address the gender question: *Markegard v. Markegard*, 616 P.2d 323 (Mont. 1980); *Kockrow v. Kockrow*, 191 Neb. 657, 217 N.W.2d 89 (1974); *Gross v. Gross*, 287 N.W.2d 457 (N.D. 1979). Still others relied on statutes that did directly address the gender question: *Martin v. Martin*, 306 N.W.2d 648 (S.D. 1981); *Fink v. Fink*, 685 P.2d 34 (Wyo. 1984); *Johnson v. Johnson*, 564 P.2d 71 (Alaska 1977), cert. denied, 434 U.S. 1048; *Arnold v. Arnold*, 604 P.2d 109 (Nev. 1979). (This last case was decided on policy grounds; the statute had been passed but had not yet taken effect when the custody decision was to be made.)

To the extent that statutory authority was correctly relied upon by these courts, responsibility for the rulings can be laid at the feet of the respective state legislatures. In such cases the analysis in the text of self-interest in the courts in these matters would be applicable to the legislative bodies involved.

24. Natural fertilization by a human male appears to be possible at least until the age of ninety-four (Seymour, Duffy, and Koerner, "A Case of Authenticated Fertility in a Man, Aged 94," 1423).

25. As explained in some detail in chapter I, above, genetic relationships are expressed in terms of fractions such as one-half, one-fourth, one-eighth, etc. These fractions refer to the degree of overlap between two individuals of familial genes, that is, genes that are relatively rare in the population as a whole, but common within a family. See generally Alexander, *Darwinism and Human Affairs*, 44, 45, 130; Dawkins, *The Selfish Gene*, 97–100; and Breuer, *Sociobiology and the Human Dimension*, 14–15.

26. O'Sullivan and Meckler, *The Draft and Its Enemies* 278–79.

27. The political climate surrounding the ending of the draft was described in 1973 by an inside observer as follows: "It is appalling that so many antiwar congressmen have climbed and stayed on the voluntary army bandwagon. . . . What turned this nation around on Vietnam was . . . the realization [by successive administrations] that the vast middle class of America would not permit *their* sons to die in a war which they considered meaningless. It was middle- and upper-class Americans who know how to contact congressmen, influence their local communities—and most all of whom vote and know finance campaigns—who posed

the sharp dilemma to Washington: get out of Vietnam or get out of office" (Califano, "Doubts About an All-Volunteer Army," 531, 533–34). The Vietnam Peace Accord was signed on Jan. 27, 1973. In March, Secretary of Defense Elliot Richardson announced that "on behalf of the administration I have advised the chairmen of the Armed Services Committees of the Senate and of the House of Representatives that it will not be necessary to extend the draft induction authority beyond its expiration date of July 1 [1973]" (House Armed Services Committee, *The All-Volunteer Force and the End of the Draft*).

28. *Hammer v. Dagenhart*, 247 U.S. 251 (1918). (Four justices dissented.) As summarized by the Court (at 269), the legislation, stripped of technical details, would "have prohibited the transportation in interstate commerce of manufactured goods, the product of a factory in which, within thirty days prior to their removal therefrom, children under the age of fourteen have been employed or permitted to work, or children between the ages of fourteen and sixteen years have been employed or permitted to work more than eight hours in any day, or more than six days in any week, or after the hour of seven o'clock p.m. or before the hour of 6 o'clock a.m. . . ."

29. "In an investigation made by the United States Census Bureau in 1905 covering 3,297,819 wage earners, the average weekly earnings of all classes was found to be $10.06 or $523.12 a year. For men above sixteen years the average was $11.16; for women $6.17, and for children under sixteen, $3.46" (Markham, Lindsey, and Creel, *Children in Bondage*, 254).

The children involved in the *Hammer v. Dagenhart* litigation were working in a cotton mill in North Carolina. "A labor commissioner of North Carolina reported that there were two hundred and sixty-one cotton mills in that State, in which nearly forty thousand people are employed, including nearly eight thousand children. The average daily wage of the men is fifty-seven cents, of the women thirty-nine cents, of the children twenty-two cents" (46).

30. "One [reason for child labor] is that children can be employed cheaper than adults and thereby their employers can make more profits out of the particular business in which they are employed" (McKellar of Tennessee during congressional debate on the legislation addressed in *Hammer v. Dagenhart*, 53 *Cong. Rec.* 2014, [1916]).

31. The solicitor general stated, in the *Hammer* case, that "The dangers to persons of tender years in working about machinery are apparent to everyone. But the evil effects on the child's physical well-being were shown by medical science to be not confined to the so-called dangerous occupations. Night work and excessive hours of labor indoors in factories at a critical stage in the development of the child's body stunt the physique and decrease the resistance to disease. The child worker becomes dwarfed in body and mind, and the state is deprived of that vigorous citizenship upon which the success of democracy must depend."

See the solicitor general's argument for the appellant in *Hammer v. Dagenhart,* 247 U.S. 251, 253-54 (1918).

32. See Sociobiology Study Group of Science for the People, *Sociobiology— Another Biological Determinism,* 280-90; Montagu, Introduction to *Sociobiology Examined;* and Sheehan, "Paris: Moses and Polytheism," 3, 12, 342. Sahlins, in his book *The Use and Abuse of Biology: An Anthropological Critique of Sociobiology,* stated that "the theory of sociobiology has an intrinsic ideological dimension, in fact a profound historical relation to Western competitive capitalism" (xii).

Cf. Masters, "Is Sociobiology Reactionary? The Political Implications of Inclusive-Fitness Theory," 275, illustrating how sociobiology "could well challenge existing sociopolitical beliefs and institutions rather than support them," and Campbell, "The Two Distinct Routes beyond Kin Selection to Ultrasociality: Implications for the Humanities and Social Sciences," 36, where the author, a psychologist, says that theorization by him and others has laid the grounds "for an explanation of the human predilections for an ideology of equality . . . as well as the liberty and fraternity that standard sociobiology may also explain."

33. See text of chapter III, supra, between note superscripts 7 and 21.

VII

Using Legal Opinions to Test
Sociobiological Hypotheses

Introduction

My purpose for engaging in the exercise contained in this chapter is to suggest that law libraries contain large amounts of data with which sociobiological hypotheses might be tested. In previous publications and in much of this book, I have demonstrated how sociobiology might be used to assist lawmakers; I focus here on the potential interrelationship of law and sociobiology *in the other direction*—assistance that the legal field might provide to scientists in their attempts to test sociobiological theory. At first glance, it may seem circular or inconsistent to suggest that a theory, when substantiated, might be used to add strength and verity to a structure like the law and then suggest that there is some strength or verity in the structure that might be used to test the theory. But consistency emerges if one looks closely at the aspects of the law and legal process that might be used to test sociobiological theory and those that might eventually benefit from the application of it. I elaborate on this at the end of the chapter, but let us move now to our primary focus.

Using U.S. Court Opinions to Test
Sociobiological Hypotheses

Scientists from various disciplines are at work testing the hypotheses of sociobiology.[1] Lawyers have an interest in the outcome of these efforts because the current consensus theory of sociobiology contains the potential for assisting lawmakers in the solution of legal problems. The use of sociobiology by lawmakers has been a subject of discussion for some time now.[2] But little thought has thus far been given to the possibility that the field of law could help scientists in their efforts to test the theory.

Specifically, I am thinking about roughly three million easily accessible reports on human transactions written by educated, experienced, and generally articulate members of U.S. society. These people might be called "elders," in a broad sense of the term, by anthropologists. The reports span over three hundred years, and uncounted numbers of them describe what the "elders" considered typical behavior of U.S. populations at the time the reports were written. These reports are indexed, and most have been summarized within subject-matter categories. I am referring to judicial opinions—the reports of cases decided by judges in governmentally established courts in the United States.

Anthropological data reporting on the behavior of various peoples in various cultures are being used to test sociobiological hypotheses.[3] The most valuable reports for such a purpose come from firsthand observations of the behavior in question, based on large scientifically selected samples. Such optimal data collection is time-consuming and expensive. When scientists go to the literature to test sociobiological hypotheses, they find few studies that satisfy stringent standards of methodology.[4] Moreover, because of the time and expense involved, new studies that satisfy such standards are likely to be slow in coming.

Studies of reports by "elders" of how the people in their societies typically behave constitute "soft" data. Reports by the informants may be consciously or unconsciously colored by idealization and personal bias. When this kind of data is used to test human behavioral hypotheses, it has been, and should be, used gingerly and only in lieu of more solid information. The information on typical behavior in U.S. case law reports must, generally speaking, be considered "soft" data.

On the other hand, these reports feature certain methodological strengths not offered by the usual anthropological "elder" data. If the subject matter involved is something that U.S. courts have been dealing with for a long time, the reports can be longitudinally strong; that is, if U.S. "elders" in 1850, 1920, and 1980 have suggested in preserved writings that the same type of behavior was typical of the populations described as of each of those dates, those writings should be more solid as data on universal, time-honored behavior than the oral reports of the elders of a society that only cover a single point in time. The researcher testing sociobiological hypotheses is particularly interested in universal, time-honored behavior.

The area of the law I have chosen for our focus in this chapter involves, among other things, surmises of "elders" (let us now call them judges) about "expectations of indebtedness" that family members have as the result of interactions between them. Scientists testing sociobiological hypotheses have paid attention to anthropological data concerning mental attitudes such as "feelings of indebtedness."[5] But reports of such subjective states of mind as "feelings" or "expectations" concerning indebtedness are relatively unreliable guides to actual behavior in a population. Scientists testing sociobiological hypotheses are primarily interested in reports of actual behavior.

Fortunately for us, in the process of deciding cases that hinge on the expectations of indebtedness of interacting family members, U.S. judges have given us their opinions as to when people living in the same household are most likely to be involved in reciprocal aid-giving relationships. These opinions constitute data on actual behavior of the populations the judges were describing, and this area of behavior—reciprocity—is at the core of sociobiological theory.

It appears to be particularly difficult for those who systematically study animal behavior to observe and report on human reciprocity in order to test sociobiological theory. Researchers who recently spent a year or more executing well-planned studies of interactions between people in Venezuelan and Trinidadian villages have suggested that considerably more time and effort would be required to identify such interactions as incidents in reciprocal aid-giving relationships.[6] Thus, scientists may find the opinion information on reciprocity in legal decisions of particular interest, at least until satisfactory direct observational studies can be mounted.

I earlier mentioned a limitation on such opinion data that is worth noting again. It will be obvious to an anthropologist, but not necessarily to other readers. When people in leadership or rule-making positions in any society give their opinions as to typical behavior in the society, there is always the possibility that their reports are consciously or unconsciously colored by idealization. They may be reporting what they think *ought* to be happening rather than what is happening.

In U.S. society legislators are charged with promulgating rules that shape conduct. Judges are, in theory, primarily charged with resolving disputes brought before them by *discovering* relevant law and facts and making decisions based upon those two elements. Conscious, overt rule-making does emerge from the judicial process, however, and one must suppose that some unconscious or disguised effort to influence conduct occurs as well.

The judicial opinion data on typical behavior is, of course, also subject to error due to individual judges' limited exposure to the phenomenon in question, faulty observation, or failure of memory. Such error may, in the case of any given judge, be more profound than those in a behavioral scientist's carefully prepared and executed observation of reciprocity in a population. But, on behalf of the judicial data, one might point out that when we have the opinions of hundreds of judges that come to the same conclusion, a corrective factor should operate as a counterbalance to reporting errors and idealization: Though one judge may have faulty observational capacities, another will be keen in that regard. Though one judge may be consciously or unconsciously idealizing "typical" behavior, another may not. This corrective factor lends some assurance that if a large number of judges has agreed on an observation of typical behavior, the observation was objectively correct.

We should note that there is another basis for possible error in the opinions of U.S. judges regarding typical behavior of the population over an extended period of time: they are sensitized to the need to follow precedent.[7] This means, in essence, that the parties in the case before the court should get the same treatment from the legal system that parties received in similar, previous cases where the facts were essentially the same. This rule of thumb focuses on the results of litigation. On essentially the same facts, if one plaintiff has won a case, the plaintiff in the next such case should also win, and the measure of what they receive should be essentially the same. If this is done, the ideal of equal justice is served.

In its strict sense, the doctrine of precedent operates only within a given jurisdiction that a court system serves. In the United States, there are currently fifty-one jurisdictions, representing each of the states, and, in addition, the federal court scheme. Thus, the state courts of Wisconsin, for example, will generally attempt to reach uniform results from case to case in those cases where Wisconsin law is applicable. In cases where no precedent exists in the state in question, however, courts will often look to cases from sister states for guidance.

It is important to emphasize that the doctrine of precedent only calls for similar *results* in similar cases. It does not suggest that observations *incidental* to the resolution of a dispute, such as observations on typical behavior of the general population, should be adhered to from case to case regardless of actual changes over time in that behavior. Nevertheless, one must allow for the possibility that some judges may have been reluctant to express their opinion that typical behavior in their jurisdiction has changed due to a generalized effect of their attempts to adhere to precedent.

However, the static effects of the doctrine of precedent have proven to be limited. As society changes, the changes have a way of eventually being reflected in judicial opinions.[8] Thus one can be reasonably sure that dozens of judges who expressed the same opinion in the late twentieth century as to the circumstances under which reciprocal aid-giving relationships are likely to arise in households in their jurisdictions did not do so simply because other judges said the same thing in another jurisdiction in 1850. I have more observations on this matter toward the end of the chapter, where I discuss methodology.

Finally, we should observe that one must be cautious when approaching case law reports for insights into typical behavior, because much of the content of such reports is directed to the conduct of the people who are before the court. These are people whose interpersonal problems were not settled without resort to an official adjudicative body—most human conflicts are resolved without such drastic measures. As the parties in court are usually displaying aberrant behavior merely by being there, it is very possible that they represent an aberrant subset in respect to other aspects of their behavior as well. Thus any judicial pronouncements directed to the behavior of the subset of the population that engages in litigation could be suspected of being atypical of the conduct of the larger population in the community.

However, on the way to resolving disputes between members of the subset that appear in court, judges often make pronouncements on typical behavior of the *general* population. It is this type of pronouncement that should be of particular interest to scientists, and it is this type that I subsequently illustrate in this chapter.

I think we can conclude now that written opinions of U.S. judges may have some value for researchers testing sociobiological hypotheses. Surely it will be worthwhile for me to lead the reader through an illustrative exercise.

The Structure of the Exercise

The body of case law upon which I will focus involves the recovery of monetary compensation for services performed by one family member for another when such services are not performed pursuant to an explicit contract. This subject parallels a key concept of sociobiology—the biology of aid-giving as it is affected by the degree of relationship between the interacting parties. This legal subject matter was the first that occurred to me when I contemplated the possibility of looking at large collections of court decisions to test sociobiological hypotheses, and it is the only one that I have pursued. There undoubtedly are many others that hold such possibilities.

The U.S. case law reports that are accessible in law libraries generally report on decisions of appellate courts in each of the states, as well as decisions of the federal court system. The usual practice has been for opinions to be written under the name of one of the several judges who constitute the panel that decides a case.

The reported court opinions relating to our subject—services performed within families—extend chronologically from at least as early as 1850 into the mid-1980s. There appear to be more than two thousand relevant opinions. It would take more than a year of a person's working hours to read and analyze these opinions thoroughly. Fortunately for this exercise, the opinions have already been read, summarized, and categorized through the years by lawyers and law professors engaged by publishing houses that specialize in that process.[9] I have used these summaries as leads to pertinent case reports. My research assistants and I have read about four hundred of the opinions that the summaries have suggested were key decisions. If scientists should decide that U.S. court decisions provide an effective testing ground for sociobiological hypotheses, a complete study of all the relevant cases in this area would be in order.

The sociobiological concepts that key into the case law we will be examining are at the core of the theory, and sociobiology may have predictive value concerning typical interactive behavior of human beings. In particular, it would permit predictions to be made as to when two people are likely to become involved in reciprocal, mutually beneficial aid-giving relationships.

In the remainder of this exercise, I first outline the relevant sociobiology. Then I present the behavioral prediction problem in the format in which it is presented to the courts and suggest predictions that sociobiologists would make about reciprocal relationships in that context. Then I describe what the court decisions have said. I end the exercise with a summary of how the legal opinions and the theory correspond and a further comment on the methodology of analyzing judicial opinions concerning typical behavior.

Relevant Sociobiological Theory

We need to concentrate, again, on sociobiological theory—this time from a perspective that will bring in, and develop more fully, the aspects that bear on the question of when reciprocal relationships can be expected to be found between people residing in the same household.[10]

Aid-Giving Exchanges

At the center of sociobiological theory is the proposition that we have been programmed by the evolutionary process to be generally predisposed toward behavior that results in the proliferation of the genes or genetic material we each carry. Having children ourselves is, of course, an effective way to proliferate our genes. But other people contain the same genetic material that we do, in varying degrees; so our genetic material can also benefit when relatives reproduce. The closer the relative, the greater the benefit.

The theory suggests that certain general aid-giving patterns have evolved in humans as accommodations of these basic concepts regarding the reproduction of our genetic material. Our personal welfare, and thus our potential to generate and nurture those with whom we have a high degree of genetic overlap, can be enhanced when we develop reciprocal relationships with other humans.[11] You scratch my back and I scratch yours—or, more to the point of this essay, you provide services and support to me when I am in need of them, and I return the favor.

For an interaction between two people to qualify as "reciprocal" there should be a minimum of two identifiable acts of aid-giving, one flowing from each side. But long-term relationships can, of course, develop, involving many such acts.

The theory suggests that we have evolved to make conscious or unconscious cost-benefit calculations before entering into and continuing reciprocal relations.[12] These calculations are based upon the likelihood that we, or our genetic material ultimately, will get at least a substantively equivalent return for the aid that we give the other party. The theory also points out that we may be adapted in appropriate circumstances to find ways to give less than a full substantive return for what we have received from the other party so that we experience a net gain. Scientists frequently call this "cheating"[13]—and let us call it that with the understanding that it does not necessarily mean a conscious, blatant, socially unacceptable effort to walk away with more than we are entitled to get. "Cheating" could also include unconscious conduct or conscious conduct that is not unduly offensive to the other party and does not rupture an ongoing relationship.[14]

For any act of beneficence, or cumulative sum of such acts, that we provide to another, there is always the possibility that we (our genetic material ultimately) will not get a substantively equivalent return. When we are interacting with a comparative stranger, the resulting deficit can be virtually complete. However, when we are dealing with close genetic relatives, we can individually get less than a full return for aid we have given them, but our genetic material can still experience a net gain because that material exists to a high degree in them as well as in us.[15] Perhaps the clearest illustration of this theoretical principle is the continuous unreciprocated aid that a mother gives her helpless infant. Even if the child reaches the age at which it is able effectively to aid others, the aid it eventually returns to its mother may never reach a substantive equivalent—yet she continues to aid the child. Fifty percent of the child's genetic material is the same as that of the mother. Thus, even though she might never receive any reciprocated aid from the child, her genetic material can benefit from her beneficence if the child reaches maturity, reproduces, and/or nurtures grandchildren or other people closely related to the mother.

The same principle operates in varying degrees between all other close relatives. The principle is called "nepotism" by sociobiologists.[16] Nepotism has another effect that is relevant for our purposes: cheating is less profitable in reciprocal arrangements with relatives than with comparative strangers. Cheating in dealings with a relative is, in "genotypic" effect, cheating oneself to the extent that one's genes overlap with that relative.[17]

Thus far in discussing sociobiological theory concerning aid-giving interactions between relatives, we have focused on close genetic relationships. Much the same behavioral tendencies I have outlined may occur between people who are closely related by marriage.[18] Sociobiologists theorize that we are predisposed to treat, with a certain diminution, in-laws "like the relative for which they are named and to which they correspond" (for example, daughter-in-law as daughter) because of the descendants these people share, or are expected to share, with us.[19] It is fairly obvious that our genetic relatives cannot reproduce our genes unless they mate with another person, so the welfare of such prospective mates should be of interest to us prior to the conceptions from such matings. Perhaps less obvious is our continuing interest in the welfare of such individuals in their capacity as nurturers of the resulting children.

I referred to a certain diminution in the treatment of in-laws as compared to the genetic relatives to which they correspond. This diminution is said to be due to the possibility that the in-laws will "defect" from our family or use their resources to aid people related to them but not to us.[20] Although many people may not have thought of their spouses as being "in-law" relatives, technically they are, when there has been a legal marriage. In any case, one's spouse is included in the theoretical concepts regarding in-laws, mentioned above,[21] and hereafter when I refer to people's "in-laws," the term will be meant to include their own spouses.

The theory I have thus far outlined constitutes a foundation from which sociobiologists will venture predictions concerning behavioral interactions between individuals. I will set out two such predictions after presenting the legal problem framework to which they are relevant. But first let me briefly explain the demographic circumstances under which scientists feel justified in making behavioral predictions based upon sociobiological theory.

Predictions from Sociobiology Based on Expansive Population Groupings

Because our ascribed behavioral predispositions interact with environment and culture, actual behavior changes as environments and cultures vary. Behavioral scientists have been working at the formidable task of trying to predict the nuances of aid-giving and cooperative behavior that are likely to occur with variations in environment and culture. Even without such theoretical refinements, however, if the population in question is large and dispersed (such as all people living in the world during the twentieth century) so that extremes of environment and culture balance each other, theorists are often confident in predicting certain behavioral patterns of the *average* individual, or two *typical* interacting individuals, under given circumstances, based primarily on presumed predispositions.

An aim of scientists testing theory regarding genetic influences on human behavior is to get as wide a view of the whole human species during as much of its history as possible. To use a metaphor from photography, the field is too vast and multidimensional to be captured in a single snapshot. One must study many samples, put them together in a composite, and then look for typical behavior in the composite.

The smaller in number, the more culturally homogeneous, and the more geographically and chronologically compacted a particular population sample is, the more likely it is to be atypical and misleading when viewed in isolation. On the other hand, the more expansive a sample is in those dimensions, the more value it has in representing typical human behavior.

The case law that we will be examining purports to reflect typical behavior fairly generally across the entire United States for more than the last hundred years. The population within that focus is not as large in number, geographically dispersed, and culturally heterogeneous as all people living in the world during the twentieth century, but it is sufficiently expansive so that—for that reason, at least—the case law we will be examining should be intriguing to scientists.

The Legal Problem

Here is a problem that has often faced the legal system:[22] A person who we will call the aid-giver, or *A*, comes into a court. He says he performed a service for another person, whom we will call the recipient, or *R*, and no one disputes that claim. *A* could have done virtually anything for *R* such as provide living quarters, shoe a horse, repair an auto, or act as a nurse for a period of time. If *R* did not request the service, he was at least aware that it was being performed. It is agreed that nothing was said about monetary compensation being paid by *R* to *A*.

A argues that the court should order *R*, or the representative of *R*'s estate if *R* is dead, to pay some reasonable amount to *A* because, *A* claims, both *A* and *R* tacitly understood and expected that *R* would pay for the service. *R* either denies that alleged "understanding" or is dead and cannot answer. Thus the court has before it a self-serving statement from one of the parties regarding subjective intention, or both parties have given such statements and they are conflicting.

A is claiming at the time of the trial, of course, that he expected monetary compensation and *R* may be in court claiming now that he did not expect to pay *A* and did not realize that *A* expected to be paid. But the issue, as the courts have framed it, involves a speculative retroactive inquiry: What did the parties intend or expect *at the time the services were performed*?[23] Their assertions at the time of trial are considered, at best, merely evidence of their states of mind at that earlier point in time. There may or may not be other indirect or "circumstantial" evidence, from the parties' conduct, as to what they intended. If such evidence exists, it may be extremely persuasive and determinative of the issue. On the other hand, it may also be conflicting and inconclusive.

It will not do for a court to excuse itself from deciding the case on the basis that the state of mind of litigants at any point in time cannot be directly discovered and that the indirect evidence before the court is of negligible value. If the court refuses to act, it will, in effect, have decided the case against the claimant who has asked the court for its help.

Thus, in order for the court to perform the dispute settlement function that has been assigned to it by society, it often needs a tie-breaker. Judges have responded to this need by announcing presumptions as to what *typical* or *average* people in the positions of A and R would have intended or expected under the circumstances.

I will reserve detailed treatment of the law until later, but we should note here that courts have said they will generally presume that monetary payment for the service was expected. However, the opposite presumption has applied when the parties were living in the same household at the time the services were rendered and were *effectively* members of the same "family," even when they were not related by blood or marriage. This is because the courts have said it was more likely than not that A and R, under such circumstances, were in an ongoing, mutually beneficial reciprocal relationship. More specifically, the courts have said that when the parties were *effectively* "family" members (even if not related) living in the same household, it was likely that R had been or was providing services or support to A, so no monetary payment was expected by the parties for the services A provided to R.

Predictions from Sociobiology Addressed to the Legal Problem

From my reading of sociobiologists, I suggest that they would, by consensus, make the following predictions concerning the likelihood of parties having an ongoing reciprocal relationship in the context of the legal problem presented. Following each proposition, I will make more informal observations on the scientific position.

When—in the U.S. population during the last one hundred years—one person, A, rendered a personal service to another person, R, while they were residing in the same household, the following would be expected:

1. *The higher the degree of "blood" relatedness between A and R, the more likely they were to have been involved together in an ongoing reciprocal aid-giving relationship.* (The term "blood" relatedness, as used by the courts, corresponds to "genetic" relatedness, used by scientists. "Most sociobiologists believe that with increasing genetic relatedness, relationships of reciprocal aid and cooperation become more probable.")[24]

2. *To the extent that A and R were close affinal relatives (in-laws), they would have been more likely to be involved in an ongoing reciprocal aid-giving relationship than if they were "complete strangers" (people having the minimal "blood" and/or affinal relationship).* (In addition to their beliefs regarding the connection between genetic relatedness and re-

lationships of reciprocal aid and cooperation noted above, "most sociobiologists . . . would agree . . . that the shared reproductive interests
of spouse and in-laws also make relationships of reciprocal aid and
cooperation more likely.")[25]

In the preamble to the above two predictions, note again the
qualification that the parties resided in the same household. This should
have particular significance for scientists. When sociobiologists have
put forward the broad proposition that humans are typically more
likely to interact with each other in aid-giving, reciprocal, or cooperative
ways the more closely they are related, they have been met with the
argument that any such interaction needs no evolutionary biological
explanation. It could be simply and completely due, it has been suggested, to the fact that relatives tend to live more closely to one another
than to other members of the population.[26] Such proximity is the
expected result of the proximity of parents and children when the latter
are born and the subsequent restraints of inertia on dispersal patterns.

This possible explanation for a tendency of close relatives to
interact has been anticipated and controlled for about as well as possible
in the above predictions. If the predictions should be borne out by
actual behavioral patterns, it is highly unlikely that the phenomena
could be entirely explained on the basis of geographic proximity of
close relatives. The effects of proximity should be essentially eliminated
because the interacting people in focus, who can be relatives *or* nonrelatives, live in the same household.[27] In other words, the universe
of the anticipated sample can be considered to consist of relatives of
varying degrees *and* other members of the population living under the
same roof.

We are prepared now to move to the judicial opinions, where we
will find that our predictions from sociobiology appear to be *uniformly*
reflected in the collective opinions of U.S. judges extending over more
than a century.

The Law Concerning Compensation
for Family Services

The courts have announced a general rule that when *A* provides
a service to *R*, with *R*'s knowledge that it is being provided, but nothing
is said by the parties regarding compensation being paid by *R* to *A*,
the law presumes that the parties intended or expected "reasonable"
compensation to be paid.[28] Presumptions such as this operate in the
law as tiebreakers when evidence on the issue in question is in equi-
poise, unclear, or nonexistent.[29] Such presumptions are said to be based

upon what the rulemakers perceive to have been typically intended or expected by people who have found themselves in similar circumstances in the past.[30] In addition to acting as a tiebreaker at the end of a trial when all the evidence has been received by the court, the presumption can be viewed and utilized as a focus or starting point for the trial of the issue.[31] If sufficient evidence is presented contrary to the presumption, it can be overcome or rebutted.[32] On the other hand, evidence may be introduced that bolsters or corroborates the presumption.[33]

Family Services Presumption

The general presumption I described above operates when the two parties involved in the provision of a service were comparative strangers.[34] The reverse presumption applies when they were not. When the parties were members of the same "family," there is a presumption that they did not expect compensation to be paid for the service rendered by A to R.[35]

The operative word "family" has a definite meaning in this context. Although there are a few opinions suggesting that the law's presumption that no compensation was to be paid applies when the parties were relatives living in separate abodes,[36] most opinions say the presumption only applies when the parties were members of the same household.[37] On the other hand, if the parties were members of the same household, they need not have been related by "blood" (as the judges say, rather than using the scientists' genetic terms), or marriage, to have been members of the same "family" for this purpose.[38] The rationale for applying the presumption that no compensation was to be paid has been variously stated,[39] but it is typified by statements that "there is a mutuality of services and advantages derived from the family relationship,"[40] that "family life abounds in acts of reciprocal kindness which tend to promote the comfort and convenience of the family,"[41] and that "the theory underlying the presumption is that support given by one is offset by services rendered by the other."[42]

Courts have often said that services or support rendered under these circumstances are presumed to be "gratuitous."[43] However, it seems clear they were using the term in the narrow sense that no *monetary* compensation was expected. If the parties were presumed by the courts not to expect monetary payment by R for a service provided by A because A and R were presumed to be in an ongoing, mutually beneficial reciprocal relationship, then the service provided by A would not be strictly "gratuitous" in the broad general sense of the term. Instead, whatever service or support A had received, or was receiving, from *R* would constitute compensation to *A*—albeit not monetary compensation.

Let us now move to the particular body of judicial opinions that correspond to the two sociobiological predictions noted earlier. In these writings judges have expressed a collective opinion that close (1) "blood" and (2) in-law relationships are positively correlated to ongoing reciprocal aid-giving bonds. The likelihood of the existence of such a bond is, as we have just noted, the basis for application of the presumption that the parties did not expect a monetary payment for the service in question. Rather than discussing the intermediate step of the relevance of blood or marriage relationships to the incidence of bonds of reciprocity, the courts have generally taken the shortcut of making pronouncements on the relevance of blood and marriage relationships to the applicability of the presumption of no expectation of monetary payment.[44] But in the following discussion of the applicability of the presumption of no expectation of monetary payment, the reader can assume, for ease of comprehension, that I am describing the presumption that a bond of reciprocity exists between the parties as the latter is the precondition to the former.

Enhanced Applicability of the Family Services Presumption when "Blood" Relatives and In-Laws Are Involved

As we have already noted, the courts have said that even unrelated parties in the same household can be "family" members so that the presumption (of no expectation of payment of compensation) is applicable in this case as well. (Sociobiologists, together with laypeople, would note here that reciprocal aid-giving bonds arise between people who are "strangers" in the sense of not being closely related by "blood" or marriage.) However, there are large numbers of opinions that express, in various ways, the point that the presumption is stronger or is more likely to be applicable when close "blood" relatives or in-laws are involved.

First, there are many opinions that contain general statements to the effect that the presumption becomes stronger the more closely "related" the parties are to one another—without being more specific as to type of relative.[45] (The relevant complete quotations from the opinions referred to in this section are set out in the notes.) Several of these opinions that speak only generally of close "relatives" have been more technical about the relationship proximity by saying that the closeness of the "degree" of the relationship has a positive bearing on the strength and applicability of the presumption.[46] (Sociobiologists would explain: not only can the reciprocal aid bond arise between people related in close degree, but the principle of nepotism enhances the likelihood that it will arise. The failure of a return to the related aid-giver is less of a loss, and the benefits from "cheating" are less, the closer the degree of the relationship.)[47]

Those courts that have made the general statements about the enhanced strength and applicability of the presumption when close "relatives" are involved probably had both "blood" relatives and in-laws in mind. To be cautious, however, we should note the possibility that some of those courts had "blood" relatives exclusively in mind. I am prompted to say this because we have found a significant number of separate decisions where courts, in discussing the applicability of the presumption, have indicated that the existence of a close "blood" relationship is an enhancing factor, without mentioning affinity relationships.[48] But the omission may have been inadvertent; "blood" relationships may merely have been uppermost in the minds of the judges when summarizing the law in this area, because most cases that get into the courts involve close genetic relationships.

Let us now look at the court statements that focus only on "blood" relatives—the subject of our first sociobiological prediction. A number of court pronouncements make the point that lack of a "blood" (meaning close genetic) relationship does not *preclude* application of the presumption.[49] It can still apply in the absence of such a relationship. These statements carry the clear implication that a close genetic relationship enhances conditions for application of the rule. Finally, and most significantly for the first sociobiological prediction, there are opinions quite directly stating the views that the presumption is strongest when close genetic relationships are involved,[50] and the closer the genetic relationship the stronger the presumption.[51]

Let us turn to our second sociobiological prediction—the one involving in-laws. As we observed, some courts have stated that the strength and applicability of the presumption were enhanced when close "relatives" were involved, and I noted the possibility that those courts had close genetic relationships exclusively in mind when using the general term "relatives." But I also noted the *probability* that most, if not all, such general statements were meant to include in-laws as well. Let me give an additional reason for that assumption. There are a significant number of separate judicial opinions explaining that the lack of a "blood" relationship or a relationship by marriage between the parties does not preclude application of the presumption.[52] This carries the clear implication that cases more easily fall *within* the rule when the parties have a close genetic *or* affinal relationship.

More importantly, there are opinions indicating quite directly that the presumption is stronger, the closer the ties of "blood" *or marriage* that exist between the parties.[53] The most explicit, particularized statement we have found on this point is one in which the court says that "[t]his presumption, which, from the very reason underlying it, must reach its highest and strongest point in the case of a child, quite as certainly and but little less strongly affects the claim of the son-in-law or daughter-in-law who joins the other marital partner in filial service to the latter's parents."[54]

Correspondence of the Law of Family Services Compensation to Sociobiological Theory

Let me extract, from the foregoing, the aspects of the law that are most important for this exercise. Over the years, U.S. courts have approached cases in which an aid-giver, A, requested the court to decree monetary compensation for A in respect to services provided to R, the recipient, when the parties had no express agreement regarding compensation, in the following manner. First, the courts have presumed that the parties did not expect monetary compensation to be paid if, at the time the services were rendered, the parties were involved in a reciprocal aid-giving bond wherein A had received, or was receiving, services from R. Second, the courts have assumed that, whatever the other aspects of the relationship between A and R, if the parties were living in the same household, conditions were conducive to such a bond of reciprocity.

Third (and this corresponds to our first sociobiological prediction), the courts have quite clearly expressed their collective opinion that, when the parties were living in the same household, the closer the "blood" relationship between A and R, the more likely it was that they were involved together in a reciprocal relationship. Fourth (and this corresponds to our second sociobiological prediction), although the pronouncements appear to be less clearly focused on the issue (perhaps because the issue has arisen less frequently),[55] the legal authorities have suggested that when there was a close in-law relationship between parties living in the same household, the existence of a bond of reciprocity was more likely than when the parties were comparative "strangers," in a "blood" or marriage relational sense.

Methodology of Analyzing Judicial Opinions Concerning Typical Behavior

Opinion data concerning typical behavior in a population can be difficult to tabulate and quantify. If interviewees can be selected on some systematic basis and then standard questions with a limited range of answers are put to the interviewees, tabulation and quantification problems will be minimal. But such problems loom large when the selection of informants is essentially accidental and those informants have had a free hand in the scope and phrasing of the information they have provided. This latter situation is what my research assistants and I have encountered in extracting information from reported judicial opinions that secondary reporting sources have suggested were most prominent in the law of family services compensation.

Of course, if all the relevant opinions on a subject are in accord, then tabulation and quantification problems dissolve to a large extent. In such a situation the major question remaining is how factually accurate the collective opinions are in portraying the behavior in question.

Among the four hundred or so opinions we have examined for this illustrative exercise, there did not appear to be any actual disagreement on the points I outlined in the last section. The opinions are phrased in different ways, and the points are developed to different extents, but all of the opinions are essentially in accord. We noticed no opinions suggesting, for example, that the closeness of "blood" or in-law relationships was irrelevant to the question of whether ongoing reciprocal aid-giving relationships were likely to exist between persons living in the same household.

We did notice a few cases that limited the operation of the presumption that depends on the likelihood that a bond of reciprocity exists—the presumption that no monetary compensation was expected for services rendered. In those cases the courts announced that they would apply the presumption only when very close "blood" relatives—parents and their children—were involved.[56] But I see no reason why these opinions are inconsistent with the two sociobiological predictions. The opinions do not suggest that the judges writing them considered more remote "blood" or in-law relationships irrelevant to the likelihood of bonds of reciprocity. These cases may simply be viewed as conservative applications of the presumption of no expectation of monetary compensation for services rendered inasmuch as that presumption is, as we noted earlier, an exception to the more general rule (presumption) that monetary compensation *is* expected when one party renders a service to another. These courts can be interpreted as having chosen to limit the application of the exception arbitrarily to parents and their children because the probable existence of a bond of reciprocity was *very* strong in such relationships.

We should note here the confounding effect that informal aspects of the U.S. court system could have on the apparent unanimity of opinions from state to state that we have found in the cases. In the sample we have examined, some seventeen state court systems are represented—from Oregon to Maryland and from North Dakota to Tennessee. In any given state, when a case first arose in which one family member sued another for compensation for services rendered, the court sitting upon the case was technically charged with declaring the law (and the social conditions calling for that law) only of the jurisdiction involved. However, it has been the practice of U.S. courts in such cases of "first impression" to look for guidance to the opinions of courts that have decided similar cases in other jurisdictions. It has been said that a decision of another state will be followed "only if the reasoning of the decision is persuasive" and "it is not against the public policy of the forum state."[57] In our sample we found several opinions that cited cases from other states when making statements relating to the effect of close genetic and in-law relationships on bonds of reciprocity.[58] Even when they did not cite such cases, the courts probably had some awareness of relevant opinions from other states. Thus there was undoubtedly some degree of cross-fertilization or contamination working in the opinions we examined.

Furthermore, once the highest court in a state makes a pronouncement on an issue, the doctrine of precedent, which I discussed in the introduction to the chapter, can result in succeeding opinions in the state reiterating the pronouncement without a thorough reexamination of the basis for it in each case.

Putting together interstate "advisement" on points of law and the doctrine of precedent, one could imagine a worst-case scenario where one court in some state in the mid-nineteenth century issues an opinion on some aspect of the behavior of citizens in its jurisdiction, which opinion is borrowed by courts in other states without reexamination and then repeated in succeeding opinions within each state, again without reexamination, resulting in a gigantic magnification, by the 1980s, of that one nineteenth-century court's opinion.

But it is extremely unlikely that such a scenario, involving any legal issue, has ever occurred in the United States. State court judges, while often seeking guidance from sister states, are notoriously independent and jealous of their prerogatives—so much so that legislative attempts to achieve uniformity in various areas of the law throughout the U.S. frequently have been thwarted when local judges have had the opportunity to interpret the "uniform" laws in their jurisdictions.[59] In view of this, the apparent uniformity of the judicial opinions we have been examining has a particular significance.

Furthermore, the doctrine of precedent, while promoting a certain static quality in legal pronouncements, has not prevented eventual change when social conditions have changed sufficiently to dictate it.[60] Thus it seems quite probable that if close blood and in-law relationships were *not* generally correlated positively to ongoing reciprocal aid relationships in the United States during the last one hundred and thirty years, it would have been noted somewhere at some time by some court dealing with lawsuits between family members in respect to services rendered. We have found no court doing so in the sample of opinions we examined.

Using the Law to Test the Theory versus Using Sociobiology to Assist Lawmakers

Before concluding this chapter I should address a somewhat collateral question that may have occurred to readers even before it was mentioned in the chapter introduction. Elsewhere, I have demonstrated how sociobiological propositions, when well established, might be used to more finely tune the law in areas where sociobiological and legal concerns overlap.[61] One might ask if it is not circular and inconsistent to suggest, as I am now doing, that the law might first be used to test sociobiological hypotheses. I suggest it is logically consistent if one clearly appreciates and distinguishes those aspects of the law and legal process that might profitably be looked to for testing from those that might be in need of fine tuning. Let me point out the differences.

We will start with the aspects of the law that could use fine tuning. Here we are focusing primarily on lawmaking under circumstances where no, or virtually no, precedent (guidance from earlier recorded experiences of lawmakers) is available. We could be talking about the drafting of a piece of innovative legislation or the writing of an innovative opinion by a judge in a case of "first impression." By way of illustration, let me sketch a scenario that may be quite similar to one that actually occurred a few years ago in the course of a legal proceeding mentioned in chapter II of this book.[62]

Assume with me that I have been appointed as a judge on a state supreme court. My benchmates and I have heard arguments in a case involving a request by an observer of a car/pedestrian accident that he be permitted to recover monetary damages, for emotional distress, from the driver of the car. Some state courts have recently been permitting such recoveries by certain close relatives of the impact victim, while other states have refused to permit any such recoveries on the grounds that emotional injuries are too easy to feign, and false claims too difficult to detect.[63] My fellow judges and I have decided to permit some recoveries of this sort in our state. We have also decided that we are going to do something that has not been done before. We will announce a rule for the future that limits such recoveries to "close" relatives of the impact victim in order to help ensure that only genuine emotional disturbances are compensated.

I have been designated as the judge to write the opinion for the court. My colleagues will look it over and may have some suggestions for changes before the opinion is published, but I am to be the principal architect of the scheme announced in the opinion—at least in respect to its finer points. Furthermore, I will be designated in the published report as the author of the opinion, so I am particularly concerned that I get things right.

In regard to the question of which observer/relatives should be permitted to recover, I have some fairly clear impressions. I have seen mothers react when their children were endangered, and to me the mothers looked essentially as frightened as if they themselves had been endangered. I also get comfort from the fact that legal authorities have been most ready permit observers to recover when they were the mothers of the impact victims.[64] Furthermore, I am a father, and I recall having severe feelings of apprehension and fright when my own child was endangered. But regarding relationships beyond mothers and fathers and their children, my impressions are vague. Any line we draw will necessarily be arbitrary but, in order to be fair, we should be consistent within our objective of helping to ensure that observer claims of emotional injury are genuine. If we permit recovery when people observe their grandparents endangered, should we permit it when the endangered one is an uncle or a niece? My vagueness here may be due, in large measure, to the fact that when relationships are more distant, my perceptual capacities regarding typical reactions of people in my community are not acute enough to give me a clear impression. One should note, also, that an individual's personal experiences and opportunities for observation are obviously limited.

Clearly I could use assistance in my efforts. I am told that socio-biological theory has something to say about typical aid-giving behavior when various relatives are involved. That may translate into typical degrees of concern for the welfare of the various relatives and, in turn, reflect the severity of emotional reactions when relatives are endangered.[65] However, I am reluctant to use pure scientific theory or even theory enjoying only minimal substantiation. If the whole of the intricate web that constitutes sociobiological theory were well substantiated, I might feel justified in applying particular aspects of it to my task.

I know that scientists are probing the theory in a piecemeal fashion by testing isolated aspects in various arenas. I would like to suggest to them that they consider using bodies of decided cases where large numbers of individual judges, over sometimes a century or more, have made pronouncements on typical behavior of U.S. populations. Collectively these judges have had considerably more experience at and opportunities for observation than any single individual. Thus, if they have all been of the same opinion regarding typical behavior, their consensus lends confidence that it was right. Perhaps such large bodies of legal opinions can assist in testing sociobiological theory. If so, and if those tests, together with others conducted with other data, eventually substantiate the theory, sociobiology may be of assistance to judges in the future who face innovative lawmaking tasks, like mine, that involve human behavioral tendencies.

Let us now return to reality, where I am not a judge but an old student of the law. I have used a fictional format, drawn upon a real current problem area, to demonstrate how a court (or legislature) entering into an uncharted, innovative area of lawmaking where little or no precedent exists could utilize sociobiological theory once it is well settled and substantiated. I have woven into the story my narrator's suggestion that, for the time being, aid might flow in the other direction. Scientists might test the theory using areas of the law that contain much recorded history in the form of lawmakers' opinions concerning human behavior.

The problem areas with which courts and legislatures must deal can be put on a spectrum from old and recurring problems (for example, contract actions between family members) to new or innovative ones (for example, suits by bystanders to recover emotional damages). Those areas toward the ends of the spectrum would seem to hold particular potential for fruitful interchanges between science and the law. As the number of opinions on a question of typical behavior increases, the data become more valuable from the scientist's standpoint. On the other hand, when the number of opinions is small, a given lawmaker facing the question has more need for "outside" assistance from the sciences.[66]

Conclusion

The analysis of large bodies of legal decisions could prove useful to scientists and beneficial to lawmakers. The scientific use (to test sociobiological hypotheses) could be immediate. Large bodies of reported decisions commenting on behavioral characteristics of the U.S. population over as much as one hundred years or more are now on the shelves in law libraries. Because of their chronological and geographical dispersion and the large numbers of individuals who typically contribute their opinions to the decisions, these case reports would appear to have more assurance of veracity than the usual information from "elders" that has been collected by anthropologists in the past.

The benefit to lawmakers from studies of legal decisions as tests of sociobiological hypotheses would derive, in turn, from any support the tests would provide to general sociobiological theory. As we noted in chapter II, sociobiology can *currently* serve to prompt empirical studies of specific legally significant typical behavior when scientists differ with lawmakers' assumptions as to what that behavior is. But, as we have also noted throughout this book, the legal process could use sociobiology directly when the latter's intricate general theoretical network has been well confirmed by empirical evidence—when patterns of typical behavior predicted by science can be taken as representing actual typical behavior without further confirming study. The empirical research needed for sociobiology to achieve such a firm position is being conducted in many fields. The purpose of this chapter has been to suggest that legal decisions be added to those fields.

I have illustrated the potential for the use of the law to test sociobiological theory with a large body of decisions concerning compensation for family services. This body of law contains pronouncements of judges regarding reciprocal aid-giving relationships, which is a type of human behavior that is particularly difficult for scientists to observe directly. The decisions would seem, on the surface, to have sufficient indication of support for certain aspects of the theory to warrant a full-scale investigation of the data by scientists—perhaps with the collaboration of lawyers. In the decisions, a large number of judges from throughout the United States have indicated that for the last one hundred years close genetic and in-law relationships have been positively correlated to ongoing reciprocal aid-giving bonds within the U.S. population. And the context addressed in the judicial opinions essentially eliminates the possibility that any such tendency of close relatives to engage each other in reciprocal relations was attributable only to their expectable patterns of geographic proximity.

There are over three million indexed American case law reports in law libraries.[67] The group of decisions concerning compensation for family services is the only body of cases that I have explored with a view toward its possible use in testing any of the various aspects of sociobiological theory. There are certainly other similar bodies of cases. Some of them could be of interest to those testing sociobiological hypotheses even if the group of cases dealing with compensation for family services is not intriguing.

NOTES

1. In this chapter I report on data regarding the effect of close genetic and in-law relationships on the likelihood of people *being involved* in ongoing reciprocal helping relationships. For an empirical study on the *direction* of helping behavior among a sample of California women and their genetic relatives, in-laws, and friends, see Essock-Vitale and McGuire, "Women's Lives Viewed from an Evolutionary Perspective II. Patterns of Helping."

   A rapidly increasing volume of reports on tests of sociobiological theory is appearing in scientific journals and anthologies. The following are a few randomly selected examples of such reports. Daly and Wilson, "Abuse and Neglect of Children in Evolutionary Perspective"; Gaulin and Schlegel, "Paternal Confidence and Paternal Investment: A Cross-Cultural Test of a Sociobiological Hypothesis"; Lenington, "Child Abuse: The Limits of Sociobiology"; Lightcap, Kurland, and Burgess, "Child Abuse: A Test of Some Predictions from Evolutionary Theory"; Littlefield and Rushton, "When a Child Dies: The Sociobiology of Bereavement"; Turke and Betzig, "Those Who Can Do: Wealth, Status, and Reproductive Success on Ifaluk"; and Betzig, *Despotism and Differential Reproduction: A Darwinian View of History.*

2. See note 1 to chapter II, supra.

3. See, e.g., Chagnon, "Mate Competition, Favoring Close Kin, and Village Fissioning among the Yanomamo Indians"; Essock-Vitale and McGuire, "Predictions Derived from the Theories of Kin Selection and Reciprocation Assessed by Anthropological Data"; and Turke and Betzig, "Those Who Can Do."

4. See Essock-Vitale and McGuire, "Predictions Derived," 238, and Kurland, "Paternity, Mother's Brother, and Human Sociality," 158.

5. Ibid.

6. Hames, "Relatedness and Interaction among the Ye'kwana: A Preliminary Analysis," 244, and Flinn, "Resources, Mating, and Kinship: The Behavioral Ecology of a Trinidadian Village," 236–37.

7. Cardozo, *The Nature of the Judicial Process*, 142.

8. Ibid., at 151: "That court best serves the law which recognizes that the rules of law which grew up in a remote generation may, in the fullness of experience, be found to serve another generation badly, and which discards the old rule when it finds that another rule of law represents what should be according to the established and settled judgment of

society . . ." (quoting J. Wheeler in *Dwy v. Connecticut Co.*, 89 Conn. 74, 99, 92 A. 883, 891 [1914]).

9. Corbin, 3 *Corbin on Contracts* §566 (1960 and Supp. 1984); S. Williston, 1 *A Treatise on The Law of Contracts* §36 (1957 and Supp. 1984); Annot., 92 *A.L.R. 3d* 726 (1979 and Supp. 1984); 66 *Am. Jur. 2d*, "Restitution and Implied Contracts," §§19–57 (1973 and Supp. 1984); 41 *Am. Jur. 2d*, "Husband and Wife," §§9, 422 (1968 and Supp. 1985); Annot., 7 *A.L.R. 2d* 8 (1949). See also Havighurst, "Services in the Home—A Study of Contracts Concepts in Domestic Relations," and Note, "Domestic Relations—the Presumption of Gratuitous Services—Must a Wife Work for Free?" 237–39.

10. See generally regarding the evolution of reciprocal relationships, Trivers, *Social Evolution*, 361–94.

11. Trivers, "The Evolution of Reciprocal Altruism."

12. Ibid.

13. E.g., ibid., 209; Alexander, "The Evolution of Social Behavior," 356; and West Eberhard, "The Evolution of Social Behavior by Kin Selection," 30.

14. Trivers, "The Evolution of Reciprocal Altruism," 209–10.

15. See, e.g., Alcock, *Animal Behavior*, 520.

16. Alexander, "The Evolution of Social Behavior," 356.

17. Ibid.

18. See Irons, "Human Female Reproductive Strategies," 200–203.

19. Alexander, *Darwinism and Human Affairs*, 159–60 (acknowledging assistance of William Irons on this point).

   See also Flinn, "Resources, Mating, and Kinship," 44: "Reciprocity among in-laws also might be more advantageous, although there are asymmetries that favor uni-directional nepotism (e.g., nepotism toward sib's spouse)." Flinn would seem to be referring to the likelihood that a person ("Ego") will be more interested in the welfare of a sib's spouse than vice versa. From Ego's standpoint the sib's spouse is in a position to generate, and have particular motivation to nurture, close genetic relatives of Ego (nieces and nephews). From sib's spouse's standpoint, Ego has some, but relatively less, motivation to nurture the same people, but any children that Ego generates will not be close genetic relatives of sib's spouse.

   The "in-laws" that the scientists are referring to here would appear to include "step-relations," and similar asymmetries may exist within those relationships. For example, from the perspective of Ego's stepchild, Ego is in a position to generate, *and* have particular motivation to nurture, people who are the stepchild's half-siblings. From Ego's perspective, the stepchild has some, but relatively less, motivation to nurture those same children, but Ego has comparatively little interest in the stepchild's generative capacities.

20. Alexander, *Darwinism and Human Affairs*, 160.

21. Flinn, "Resources, Mating, and Kinship," 44: "Long-term reciprocal commitments among affinal relatives (those linked by a mating relationship,

e.g., in-laws) are dependent upon the probability that the mating relationship will be maintained. The most important affinal relatives are
mates."

Regarding the treatment of spouses under the law concerning compensation for services rendered within the family see note 55, infra.

22. See generally the authorities listed in note 9, supra.
23. See *Newbert v. McCarthy*, 190 Cal. 723, 725, 214 Pa. 442, 443 (1923);
    Payne v. Bank of Am. Nat'l Trust and Sav. Ass'n, 128 Cal. App. 2d 295,
    304, 275 P.2d 128, 134 (1954). See also, e.g., *Seals v. Edmondson*, 73 Ala.
    295, 298 (1882); *Kellum v. Browning's Adm'r*, 231 Ky. 308, 315, 21 S.W.2d
    459, 463 (1929).
24. William Irons, in a letter to the author (Aug. 21, 1985). See Alexander,
    "The Evolution of Social Behavior," 356; Flinn, "Resources, Mating, and
    Kinship," 36–37; and West Eberhard, "The Evolution of Social Behavior,"
    19. See also Hames, "Relatedness and Interaction," 247. (Patterns of
    reciprocity vary according to the amount of "relatedness" shared by the
    individuals interacting.)
25. Irons, letter to author. See also the authorities cited in note 19, supra.
26. "[O]ne might argue that interaction is a function of residential propin-
    quity, in that people who are closely related to one another, such as
    nuclear family members, tend to live in the same house, and therefore
    their rates of interaction would be greater than those with people who
    live in different houses" (Hames, "Relatedness and Interaction," 246).
    Hames is here reflecting the position of critics like Marshall Sahlins.
    (See Sahlins, *The Use and Abuse of Biology*.) Hames goes on to present
    evidence from his study of the Ye'kwana that "even when the effects
    of propinquity are controlled, interaction still varies predictably with
    relatedness" (ibid., 247).
27. "[I]t would be desirable to negate or control the effects of propinquity
    on interaction in order to test the effects of relatedness alone on inter-
    action" (ibid).
28. *Yeats v. Moody*, 128 Fla. 658, 661–62, 175 So. 719, 720 (1920); *Symon v.
    Davis*, 245 So.2d 278, 279 (Fla. Dist. Ct. App. 1971); *Shurrum v. Watts*,
    80 Idaho 44, 51, 324 P.2d 380, 384 (1958); *Weber v. Eastern Idaho Packing
    Corp.*, 94 Idaho 694, 697, 496 P.2d 693, 696 (1972).
29. "In other words, the acceptance of valuable services or materials raises
    a presumption of intent to pay, or expectation of payment, or presumption
    that the services were to be compensated, or a presumption of legal
    liability or obligation, or there is a presumption that payment of com-
    pensation is at least implied; and the presumption is sufficient to throw
    on the person contesting liability the burden of showing an agreement
    indicating that the services were to be gratuitous, or that the circum-
    stances surrounding the transaction were such that no reasonable person
    would expect payment." See 98 *C.J.S.*, "Work and Labor," 10 (1957).
30. See Corbin, 3 *Corbin on Contracts*, 288–90.
31. *Disbrow v. Durand*, 54 N.J.L. 343, 345, 24 A. 545, 546 (1892).

32. 66 *Am. Jur. 2d* §§40, 42 (1973); Havighurst, "Services in the Home," 393.

33. 66 *Am. Jur. 2d* §41 (1973).

34. See *In re Foster's Estate*, 46 Ill. App. 2d 319, 326, 197 N.E.2d 257, 260 (1964); *In re Holta's Estate*, 246 Iowa 527, 531, 68 N.W.2d 314, 317 (1955); *Kalavros v. Deposit Guar. Bank & Trust Co.*, 248 Miss. 107, 118, 158 So.2d 740, 744 (1963); *In re Fox's Estate*, 131 W. Va. 429, 433, 48 S.E.2d 1, 4 (1948).

35. E.g., *Collard v. Cooley*, 92 Idaho 789, 793, 451 P.2d 535, 539 (1969); *Shurrum v. Watts*, 80 Idaho 44, 51, 324 P.2d 380, 384 (1958); *Meyer v. Meyer*, 379 Ill. 97, 103–4, 39 N.E.2d 311, 314 (1942); *In re White*, 15 Ill. App. 3d 200, 201, 303 N.E.2d 569, 571 (1973); *In re Estate of Thacker*, 152 W.Va. 455, 464, 164 S.E.2d 301, 307 (1968); *In re Fox's Estate*, 131 W. Va. 429, 433, 48 S.E.2d 1, 4 (1948). See also *In re Wetmore*, 36 Ill. App. 3d 96, 98, 343 N.E.2d 224, 225 (1976).

36. See *Weir v. Carter's Estate*, 224 S.W. 147, 150 (Mo. Ct. App. 1920); *In re Taylor's Estate*, 132 Wis. 38, 44, 111 N.W. 229, 232 (1907); *Williams v. Williams*, 114 Wis. 79, 84, 89 N.W. 835, 836 (1902).

37. *Bemis v. Bemis*, 83 Ohio App. 95, 100, 82 N.E.2d 757, 759–60 (1948); *Brown v. Cummings*, 27 R.I. 369, 369–70, 62 A. 378, 379 (1905). See *Jessup v. Jessup*, 17 Ind. App. 177, 185–86, 46 N.E. 550, 552 (1897); *Jaycox v. Brune*, 434 S.W.2d 539, 544 (Mo. 1968); *Steva v. Steva*, 332 S.W.2d 924, 926-27 (Mo. 1960); *Brassfield v. Allwood*, 557 S.W.2d 674, 681 (Mo. 1977); *Sturgeon v. Wideman*, 608 S.W.2d 140, 141-42 (Mo. Ct. App. 1980); *In re Galtz*, 205 Wis. 590, 594, 238 N.W. 374, 376 (1931); *Fuerst v. Fuerst*, 286 N.W.2d 861, 867 (Wis. Ct. App. 1979).

38. *Crampton v. Logan*, 28 Ind. App. 405, 407–8, 63 N.E. 51, 52 (1902); *Pearre v. Smith*, 110 Md. 531, 534, 73 A. 141, 142 (1909); *Harper v. Davis*, 115 Md. 349, 354, 80 A. 1012, 1014 (1912); *Manning v. Driscoll's Estate*, 174 S.W.2d 921, 924 (Mo. Ct. App. 1943); *Nelson v. Poorman's Estate*, 215 S.W. 753, 754 (Mo. Ct. App. 1919); *Disbrow v. Durand*, 54 N.J.L. 343, 345, 24 A. 545, 546 (1892); *In re McDonald's Estate*, 4 N.J. Misc. 542, 545–46, 133 A. 884, 885 (1926); *Ratliff v. Sadlier*, 53 Nev. 292, 301, 299 P. 674, 676 (1931); *Franklin v. Northrup*, 107 Or. 537, 550, 215 P. 494, 499 (1923); *Lawrence v. Ladd*, 290 Or. 181, 194, 570 P.2d 638, 644 (1977); *York v. Place*, 273 Or. 947, 949, 544 P.2d 572, 574 (1975). See also *Gjurich v. Fieg*, 164 Cal. 429, 432, 129 P. 464, 465 (1913).

39. See, e.g., the following excerpts: *Williams v. Walden*, 82 Ark. 136, 142–43, 100 S.W. 898, 900–901 (1907) (A son's services for his father are gratuitous, "enjoined by the reciprocal duties of the family relation."); *Snyder v. Nixon*, 188 Iowa 799, 781, 176 N.W. 808, 809 (1920) (Family "duties are reciprocal, and the services are presumed to be reciprocal."); *Squire's Estate*, 168 Iowa 597, 608, 150 N.W. 706, 710 (1915) ("The obligation between all members of the family is reciprocal."); *Disbrow v. Durand*, 54 N.J.L. 343, 345, 24 A. 545, 546 (1892) ("[T]he household family relationship is presumed to abound in reciprocal acts of kindness and good will. . . ."); and *Williams v. Hutchinson*, 3 N.Y. 312, 318 (1850)

(Between family members, "[w]e find other motives than the desire of gain which may prompt the exchange of mutual benefits between them. . . .").

40. *Kleinhesselink's Estate,* 230 Iowa 1090, 1094, 300 N.W. 315, 317 (1941).

41. *Key v. Harris,* 116 Tenn. 161, 171, 92 S.W. 235, 237 (1905).

42. *Johnston v. Johnston,* 182 Wash. 573, 575, 47 P.2d 1048, 1049 (1935). Cf. *Ferris v. Barrett,* 250 Iowa 646, 95 N.W.2d 527 (1959) (A claimant was permitted to recover for services performed in case where recipient could not reciprocate).

43. *Meyer v. Meyer,* 379 Ill. 97, 103-4, 39 N.E.2d 311, 314 (1942); *Youngberg v. Holstrum,* 252 Iowa 815, 822, 108 N.W.2d 498, 502 (1961); *In re Talty's Estate,* 232 Iowa 280, 283, 5 N.W.2d 584, 586 (1942); *Snyder v. Guthrie,* 193 Iowa 624, 628, 187 N.W. 953, 955 (1922); *Bryant v. Stringer,* 183 So.2d 895, 899 (Mo. 1966).

44. "Most presumptions have come into existence primarily because the judges have believed that proof of fact B renders the inference of the existence of fact A so probable that it is sensible and timesaving to assume the truth of fact A until the adversary disproves it" (McCormick, *McCormick on Evidence,* 969).

45. *Nashville Trust Co. v. Commissioner,* 136 F.2d 148, 151 (6th Cir. 1943) ("While . . . a presumption of gratuitous service extends to all relatives living in the same family group, it grows weaker and becomes more easily rebutted as the relationship recedes" [citation omitted]); *Quigly v. Harold,* 22 Ill. App. 269, 270-71 (1887) ("[W]here one lives with and performs services for a near relative the presumption arises such services were intended to be gratuitous, yet, in such cases the more distant the relationship the weaker such presumption. . . ."); *In re Talty's Estate,* 232 Iowa 280, 287, 5 N.W.2d 584, 588 (1942) ("The presumption of gratuity ordinarily is less strong as the relationship between the parties becomes more remote." [citation omitted]); *Shane v. Smith,* 37 Kan. 55, 58, 14 P. 477, 479 (1887) ("The nearer the relation the stronger the presumption . . . , the more distant the relation the weaker the presumption that [the parties] are to be treated as members of the same family."); *Gorrell v. Taylor,* 107 Tenn. 568, 570-71, 64 S.W. 888, 888 (1901) ("And the presumption of gratuitous service goes beyond the real blood relation of parent and child. It extends . . . , indeed, to all relatives living together in the same family; but it naturally grows weaker, and therefore becomes more easily rebutted, as the relationship recedes."); and *In re Kessler's Estate,* 87 Wis. 660, 666, 59 N.W. 129, 131 (1924) ("As between remote relatives, at least, there is great reason for holding that the presumption that the services were intended to be gratuitous is relatively weakened. . . ." [citation omitted]). See *Thornton v. Grange,* 66 Barb. 507, 509 (N.Y. 1873) ("When, however, the person taken into the family is not a child, but a more distant relation, the presumption of serving without pay is less strong. . . ." [citation omitted]); *Cotton v. Robert's Estate,* 47 Tenn. App. 277, 285, 337 S.W.2d 776, 780 (1960) ("[A]s to services

performed . . . on behalf of another member of the same family, there is a presumption, which grows weaker as the relationship recedes, that the services are rendered gratuitously. . . ." [citation omitted]).

46. *Hartley v. Bohrer*, 52 Idaho 72, 76–77, 11 P.2d 616, 617 (1932) ("[T]he degree of relationship may strengthen or diminish the implication that the services are acts of gratuitous kindness or affection according to its proximity or remoteness."); *In re Estate of Dal Paos*, 118 Ill. App. 2d 235, 240, 254 N.E.2d 300, 303 (1960) ("The presumption diminishes in direct proportion to the remoteness of the degree and character of the family relationship. . . ." [citation omitted]); *Smith v. Myers*, 19 Mo. 433, 435 (1854) ("In all such [family service] cases, it will be a question for the jury, taking into consideration the nature and degree of the relationship . . . , whether there was any implied contract for compensation. The degree of the relationship may strengthen or diminish the implication, according to its proximity or remoteness."); *Penter v. Roberts*, 51 Mo. App. 222, 227 (1892) (quotes the language used by the *Smith* court, supra); and *In re Baker's Estate*, 144 Neb. 797, 801–2, 14 N.W.2d 585, 589 (1944) ("The presumption of gratuity . . . is entirely rebuttable . . . , and such presumption diminishes in direct proportion to the remoteness of the degree and nature of the family relationship. . . ."). Cf. the following opinions, which list "degree of kinship" or "degree of relationship" among the factors to be considered in family service compensation cases: *Kellum v. Browning's Adm'r*, 231 Ky. 308, 323–24, 21 S.W.2d 459, 467 (Ct. App. 1929); *Whaley v. Peak*, 49 Mo. 80, 83 (1871); and *In re Estate of Paketti*, 340 N.W.2d 894, 901–2 (N.D. 1983).

47. The textual statement should hold for in-law relationships, as well as close genetic relationships, in spite of the asymmetries involved in in-law relationships. See supra, note 19.

48. E.g., *Staples' Ex'r v. Barrett*, 242 S.W.2d 996, 998 (Ky. Ct. App. 1951) ("[Though these parties are unrelated] the various degrees of consanguinity are also facts which [usually] must be graded and appraised in connection with those from which the contract is sought to be implied."). See also all of the opinions cited infra in notes 50 and 51.

49. *De Fevers' Ex'r v. Brooks*, 203 Ky. 606, 610, 262 S.W. 976, 978 (1924), ("[I]n cases of such mutual family or domestic relationships, there will be no *implied* contract for services personal to the decedent, whether the performer of them be a stranger or a blood relative." [emphasis in original]); *Disbrow v. Durand*, 54 N.J.L. 343, 345, 24 A. 545, 546 (1892) ("[The presumption may be operative in the case of a family] composed of remote relations, and even of persons between whom there is no tie of blood."); *Anderson v. Haupt*, 43 Ohio App. 538, 542, 184 N.E. 29, 30 (1932) ("It has been held that no contract to pay for services as between parties occupying family relationship will be implied even though the performer is a stranger and not blood relative." [citation omitted]); and *In re Weide's Estate*, 73 S.D. 448, 451–52, 44 N.W.2d 208, 210 (1950) ("The lack of blood relationship is admissible as a circumstance bearing

on the question of family relationship, but it is not conclusive." [citations omitted]). See also the opinions cited infra in note 52, where "blood" relationships are mentioned in this regard together with relationships by marriage.

50. *Oliver v. Gardner*, 192 Ky. 89, 92, 232 S.W. 418, 420 (1921) ("In such [domestic relationship/mutual services] cases the law presumes the services claimed for were gratuitously rendered, and especially so where near blood relationship exists. . . ."); *Vanover v. Vanover*, 252 Ky. 308, 312, 67 S.W.2d 21, 23 (1934) (quotes the language used by the *Oliver* court, supra); *Patterson v. Estate of Patterson*, 189 N.W.2d 601, 604 (Iowa 1971) ("Where there is no blood relationship, the presumption of gratuity is less strong." [citation omitted]). See also *In re Talty's Estate*, 232 Iowa 280, 287, 5 N.W.2d 584, 588 (1942) ("There was no blood relationship between [the parties]. The presumption . . . ordinarily is less strong as the relationship between the parties becomes more remote." [citation omitted]) and the opinions cited infra in note 53, where "blood" relationships are mentioned in this regard together with relationships by marriage.

51. *Quigly v. Harold*, 22 Ill. App. 269, 271 (1887) ("[T]he more distant the relationship the weaker such presumption, and it would not have the force . . . where the parties are uncle and niece, that it would have where they are parent and child. . . .").

52. *In re Estate of White*, 15 Ill. App. 3d 200, 202, 303 N.E.2d 569, 571 (1973) ("The family relationship which gives rise to the presumption need not necessarily be one of kindred. . . . [S]uch a family may exist although composed of remote relations, and even of persons between whom there is no tie of blood or affinity." [citations omitted]); *Robinson v. Johnson*, 119 Kan. 639, 639, 240 P. 962, 962 (1925) ("The rule is familiar that, even in the absence of any relationship by blood or marriage, there is no implication of a promise to pay for domestic services rendered by one who is a member of the household." [citations omitted]); *Harper v. Davis*, 115 Md. 349, 354, 80 A. 1012, 1014 (1911) ("Even in cases where the [parties] were not related by either blood or marriage, [the presumption will apply when] there existed between them a domestic relationship . . . essentially similar to those . . . between kinsfolk." [quoting *Hodge v. Hodge*, 11 L.R.A. (N.S.) 887]); and *In re Estate of Bowman*, 102 Ohio App. 121, 123, 141 N.E.2d 499, 502 (1956) ("[T]he rule [presumption of gratuity] is not confined to cases in which there is a blood relationship,—or even to relationship by marriage. A person may be a member of the family within that rule although the performer is a stranger and not a blood relative or one by marriage." [quoting 42 *Ohio Jurisprudence*, 493, Section 12]). See *People's Nat'l Bank v. Cohn*, 194 Ark. 1098, 1102, 110 S.W.2d 42, 45 (1937) ("[I]t is said that [the presumption] applies where the family relationship actually existed between claimant and decedent, although there was no consanguinity, affinity, or adoption." [citation omitted]).

53. *Crampton v. Logan*, 28 Ind. App. 405, 407–8, 63 N.E. 51, 52 (1902) ("This presumption affecting members of a household applies to all who actually live together as a family, however related, or whether related, or not, by blood or affinity. . . ."); *Ferris v. Barrett*, 250 Iowa 646, 652, 95 N.W. 2d 527, 531 (1959) ("The presumption of gratuity is very strong as between husband and wife and parent and child. In other family relationships such as sister and brother-in-laws, uncle, aunt, brother, sister and cousin, it is not of as great weight as within the intimate family circle." [citations omitted]); *Hill v. Hill*, 121 Ind. 255, 260, 23 N.E. 87, 88-89 (1889) ("The true rule is that where near relatives, either by blood or marriage, reside together . . . , the presumption may be strong or weak, owing to the degree of relation and intimacy between the parties. . . ."); *Collins v. Williams*, 21 Ind. App. 227, 229-30, 52 N.E. 92, 92-93 (1898) (quotes the language used by the *Hill* court, supra); and *Fitzpatrick v. Dooley*, 112 Mo. App. 165, 171, 86 S.W. 719, 721 (1905) ("Ties growing out of either consanguinity or marriage are factors bearing with more or less weight, according to their degree, on the inquiry of whether or not a family relation existed." [citation omitted]). See also *James v. Gillen*, 3 Ind. App. 472, 477, 30 N.E. 7, 9 (1892) ("Nearness of kinship is influential only in determining whether the family relationship does in fact exist; but, after such relationship is once established, and the parties live as members of a common family, the rule is the same, regardless of the questions of consanguinity or affinity."); *In re Estate of Bowman*, 102 Ohio App. 121, 123, 141 N.E.2d 499, 502 (1956) ("Close relationship, by blood or marriage, although the dominant consideration, is not alone sufficient to establish a family relationship. . . ."); *Lawrence v. Ladd*, 280 Or. 181, 194, 570 P.2d 638, 644 (1977) ("[T]his principle [presumption of gratuitous services] extends beyond relatives or spouses. . . ." [citation omitted]); *York v. Place*, 273 Or. 947, 949, 544 P. 572, 574 (1975) (quotes the language used by the *Franklin* court, *infra*); *Franklin v. Northrup*, 107 Or. 537, 550, 215 P. 494, 499 (1923) ("[T]he implication of a promise to pay for such services does not arise where the parties are related by blood or marriage and are members of the same family and household. . . ."); and *In re Goltz*, 205 Wis. 590, 594, 238 N.W. 374, 376 (1931) ("The law is well established that 'where near relatives by blood or marriage reside together as one common family, and one of them renders services to another, and such other furnishes him board and lodging or other necessaries or comforts, a presumption arises that neither party intended to receive or to pay compensation. . . .' " [*quoting Estate of Kessler*, 87 Wis. 660, 664, 59 N.W. 129, 130 (1924)]).

54. *Gorrell v. Taylor*, 107 Tenn. 568, 64 S.W. 888 (1901). Cf. *Ferris v. Barrett*, 250 Iowa 646, 653-54, 95 N.W.2d 527, 532 (1959) ("The sister-in-law was not a blood relative of claimant so that the presumption is not of as much weight as if she were within the intimate family circle.").

55. One gets the impression from reading the authorities (see supra note 9)

that genetic relatives and spouses constitute the bulk of "family" members who have sued in American courts to recover compensation for services rendered to one another when there was no explicit agreement regarding such compensation. See *Disbrow v. Durand*, 54 N.J.L. 343, 345, 24 A. 545, 546 (1892): "The great majority of cases [where the presumption of no expectation of monetary payment for services has been applied] have been between children and their parents, or the representatives of the parents' estate. . . ."

Cases involving spouses tend to be categorized separately from those involving other family members and are analyzed under special concepts that have developed around spousal relations. Nevertheless, it appears that essentially the same ultimate treatment is accorded to support and services provided by one spouse to the other when there is no explicit agreement for compensation as would be accorded to them under principles that are applied to other close relatives. See 41 *Am. Jur. 2d*, "Husband and Wife," §§9, 422 (1968 and Supp. 1985); Note, "Domestic Relations—The Presumption of Gratuitous Services—Must a Wife Work for Free?" 235, 237–39.

56. *Smith v. Mulligan*, 43 Pa. 107, 109 (1862). See *In re Gibb's Estate*, 266 Pa. 485, 487, 110 A. 236, 237 (1920); *Fondelier v. Riddel*, 152 Pa. Super. 586, 588, 33 A.2d 86, 87 (1943); *Gerz v. Weber*, 162 Pa. 530, 536, 29 A. 761, 763 (1894). See also *Horton's Appeal*, 94 Pa. 62, 64 (1892), and *Miller's Appeal*, 100 Pa. 568, 571 (1882). In *Peter v. Poro's Estate*, 96 Vt. 95, 103, 117 A. 244, 247 (1922), the court refused to treat, for this purpose, brothers and sisters the same as they would parents and children, although, as scientists will note, the former are, on the average, related in the same degree as the latter. See Alexander, *Darwinism and Human Affairs*, 44–45.

57. 20 *Am. Jur. 2d*, "Courts," §203 (1965): "The decision of a court of one American state does not have stare decisis effect in the court of another American state. Such a decision may be considered if it appears to throw light on the question in issue, but it will be followed only if the reasoning of the decision is persuasive. It will certainly not be followed where it is against the public policy of the forum state" (citations omitted).

58. See supra, notes 45 through 54.

59. See, e.g., Eaton, "On Uniformity in Judicial Decisions of Cases Arising Under the Uniform Negotiable Instruments Act," where the author critiques a series of cases, not to show that they are erroneous, "but to show that they ignore the uniform law on their statute books and the decisions under it" (95).

60. See supra, note 8.

61. See generally Beckstrom, *Sociobiology and the Law*.

62. *Barnhill v. Davis*, 300 N.W.2d 104 (Iowa 1981), where the Iowa Supreme Court limited the people who could recover in Iowa courts for emotional damages suffered from observing a tortious impact upon another to cases

where "[t]he bystander and the victim were husband and wife or related within the second degree of consanguinity or affinity" (108).

63. See Beckstrom, *Sociobiology and the Law*, 99–100.
64. See cases cited ibid., 114 n. 3, and see Prosser, *Law of Torts*, 334.
65. Beckstrom, *Sociobiology and the Law*, 102–13, 115 n. 25.
66. Furthermore, there will be areas of the law where considerable bodies of opinions on typical behavior exist that are of questionable value from the standpoint of lawmakers approaching the area for the first time. For example, Anglo-American jurisdictions have been producing intestate succession laws for centuries. Those laws purport, inter alia, to reflect the desires of people who die without wills as to the distribution of their property after their death. These laws, in effect, "write" the typical will of people who die without one. Of course, no one has ever observed a will of someone who died without writing one! Thus opinions of legislative drafters as to the contents of such hypothesized wills cannot be based on observational experience, so even though there is a large cumulation of such opinions, new legislative drafters entering the field may find them suspect, and welcome outside assistance in attempting to predict what people who die without a will in the future would want done with their property. Sociobiological theory, when well substantiated, may eventually offer such assistance. See Beckstrom, *Sociobiology and the Law*, 7–92.
67. Cohen and Berring, *How to Find the Law*, 99.

Epilogue

I believe we have explored a field with exciting possibilities for cross-fertilization between "pure," or academic, science and the more pragmatic world of legal affairs. Considerable space in this book has been devoted to the potential benefits to scientists from the interaction and to limitations on benefits to the legal process. Any reader wishing more detail on the potential benefits to the legal process might consult my earlier book, *Sociobiology and the Law*, which is devoted principally to that theme. I am certain that as increasing numbers of people become familiar with both the law and the science involved, much more will be discovered in the field of overlap than I have been able to locate and outline in the two books I have written on the subject.

How can the interdisciplinary learning that is necessary for such further development be fostered? Independent study is, of course, possible and should be encouraged. But the most promising route, I suggest, is through graduate degree programs where academics interested in the overlap of law and behavioral science encourage graduate students to select theses topics in the area. Such a program could result in two people becoming versed in the field—the graduate student and the student's supervisor, who must read in order to supervise.

I have tried to show where such interdisciplinary learning can lead. Although scientific researchers may benefit from familiarity with the law and cooperation with lawyers in testing behavioral hypotheses, the ultimate pay-off from a cross-fertilization of law and science here will come when information about human behavior—that can be used in solving legal problems—is produced by scientists.

Literature Cited

Alcock, J. *Animal Behavior: An Evolutionary Approach* (3d ed.). 1984.

Alexander, R. D. "The Evolution of Social Behavior." 5 *Ann. Rev. Ecology & Systematics* 325 (1974).

———. "The Search for a General Theory of Behavior." 20 *Behavioral Sci.* 77 (1975).

———. "Natural Selection and Societal Laws." In *Morals, Science and Sociality*, ed. H. Engelhardt, Jr. and D. Callahan. 1978.

———. *Darwinism and Human Affairs.* 1979.

———. "Evolution and Culture." In *Evolutionary Biology and Human Social Behavior*, ed. N. Chagnon and W. Irons. 1979.

———. "Biology and Law." 7 *Ethology & Sociobiology* 19 (1986).

———. *The Biology of Moral Systems.* 1987.

American Jurisprudence 2d. "Courts" (1965).

———. "Husband and Wife" (1968).

———. "Jury." (1969).

Areen, J. *Cases and Materials on Family Law (2d ed.).* 1985.

Asser, C. *Handleiding Tot De Beoefening Van Het Nederlands Burgerlijk Recht.* 1953.

Ball, J. "Memes as Replicators." 5 *Ethology & Sociobiology* 145 (1984).

Baran, A., A. Sorosky, and R. Pannor. "The Dilemma of Our Adoptees." *Psychology Today*, Dec. 1975, at 38.

Barash, D. P. *Sociobiology and Behavior.* 1977.

———. *The Whisperings Within.* 1979.

———. *Sociobiology and Behavior* (2d ed.). 1982.

———. *The Hare and the Tortoise: Biology, Culture and Human Nature.* 1986.

Beckstrom, J. "Sociobiology and Intestate Wealth Transfers." 76 *Nw. U.L. Rev.* 216 (1981).

———. "Die Elterliche Fürsorge Als Entscheidungskriterium in Sorgerechtsverfahren (Practical Legal Applications of Sociobiology: The Solicitude Factor in Interparental Child Custody Disputes)." In *Der Beitrag de Biologie zu Fragen von Recht und Ethik,* ed. M. Gruter and M. Rehbinder. 1983.

―――. "The Potential Dangers and Benefits of Introducing Sociobiology to Lawyers." 79 *Nw. U.L. Rev.* 1279 (1984/85).

―――. *Sociobiology and the Law: The Biology of Altruism in the Courtroom of the Future.* 1985.

―――. "Behavioral Research on Aid-Giving That Can Assist Lawmakers While Testing Scientific Theory." 1 *J. Contemp. Health L. & Policy* 25 (1986).

Bermant, G. "Sexual Behavior: Hard Times with the Coolidge Effect." In *Psychological Research: The Inside Story,* ed. M. Siegel and H. Zeigler. 1976.

Betzig, L. *Despotism and Differential Reproduction: A Darwinian View of History.* 1986.

Boorman, S., and P. Levitt. *The Genetics of Altruism.* 1980.

Boyd, R., and P. J. Richerson. *Culture and the Evolutionary Process.* 1985.

Brandon, R., and R. Burian, eds. *Genes, Organisms, Populations: Controversies over the Units of Selection.* 1984.

Breuer, G. *Sociobiology and the Human Dimension.* 1982.

Buck, R., R. Parke, and M. Buck. "Skin Conductance, Heart Rate, and Attention to the Environment in Two Stressful Situations." 18 *Psychonomic Sci.* 95 (1970).

Bureau of Census, U.S. Department of Commerce. *Historical Statistics of the United States, Colonial Times to 1970.* 1975.

―――. *Statistical Abstract of the United States: 1986* (106th ed.). 1985.

Bourne, P. "Military Psychiatry and the Vietnam Experience." 127 *Am. J. Psychiatry* 481 (1970).

Califano, J. "Doubts About an All-Volunteer Army." 1973. Reprinted in *The Military Draft,* ed. M. Anderson. 1982.

Campbell, D. "The Two Distinct Routes beyond Kin Selection to Ultrasociality: Implications for the Humanities and Social Sciences." In *The Nature of Prosocial Development: Theories and Strategies,* ed. D. Bridgeman. 1983.

Cardozo, B. *The Nature of the Judicial Process.* 1921.

Cassetty, J., ed. *The Parental Child-Support Obligation: Research, Practice, and Social Policy.* 1982.

Cavilli-Sforza, L., and M. Feldman. *Cultural Transmission and Evolution.* 1981.

Certoma, G. *The Italian Legal System.* 1985.

Chagnon, N. "Mate Competition, Favoring Close Kin and Village Fissioning among the Yanomamo Indians." In *Evolutionary Biology and Human Social Behavior,* ed. N. Chagnon and W. Irons. 1979.

―――. "Terminological Kinship, Genealogical Relatedness and Village Fissioning among the Yanomamo Indians." In *Natural Selection and Social Behavior,* ed. R. Alexander and D. Tinkle. 1981.

Chambers, D. *Making Fathers Pay: The Enforcement of Child Support.* 1979.

Cohen, M., and R. Berring. *How to Find the Law* (8th ed.). 1983.

Cohen, S. "Aftereffects of Stress on Human Performance and Social Behavior: A Review of Research and Theory." 88 *Psychological Bull.* 82 (1980).

Congress and the Nation. 1980.

Congressional Record. 1916.

Congressional Quarterly Almanac. 1981.

Congressional Quarterly Almanac. 1983.

Corbin, A. *Corbin on Contracts.* 1960.

Corpus Juris Secundum. "Juries." 1947.

————. "Work and Labor." 1957.

Daly, M., and M. Wilson. "Abuse and Neglect of Children in Evolutionary Perspective." In *Natural Selection and Social Behavior,* ed. R. Alexander and D. Tinkle. 1981.

————. *Sex, Evolution, and Behavior* (2d ed.). 1983.

————. *Homicide.* 1988.

Dawkins, R. *The Selfish Gene.* 1976.

————. *The Extended Phenotype.* 1982.

————. "Opportunity Costs of Inbreeding." 6 *Behavioral & Brain Sci.* 105 (1983).

————. *The Blind Watchmaker.* 1986.

Demarest, W. "Does Familiarity Necessarily Lead to Erotic Indifference and Incest Avoidance because Inbreeding Lowers Reproductive Fitness?" 6 *Behavioral & Brain Sci.* 106 (1983).

Drinan, R. "The Loving Decision and the Freedom to Marry." 29 *Ohio St. L.J.* 358 (1968).

Dunham, A. "The Method, Process and Frequency of Wealth Transmission at Death." 30 *U. Chi. L. Rev.* 241 (1963).

Durham, W. "Toward a Coevolutionary Theory of Human Biology and Culture." In *Evolutionary Biology and Human Social Behavior,* ed. N. Chagnon and W. Irons. 1979.

Eaton, A. "On Uniformity in Judicial Decisions of Cases Arising under the Uniform Negotiable Instruments Act." 12 Mich. L. Rev 89 (1913).

Edel, A. "Attempts to Derive Definitive Moral Patterns from Biology." 1955. Reprinted in *The Sociobiology Debate,* ed. A. Caplan. 1978.

Einstein, A. *Out of My Later Years.* 1950.

Elliott, E. D. "The Evolutionary Tradition in Jurisprudence." 85 *Colum. L. Rev.* 38 (1985).

Epstein, R. "A Taste for Privacy? Evolution and the Emergence of a Naturalistic Ethic." 9 *J. Legal Stud.* 665 (1980).

Essock-Vitale, S., and M. McGuire. "Predictions Derived from the Theories of Kin Selection and Reciprocation Assessed by Anthropological Data." 1 *Ethology & Sociobiology* 233 (1980).

————. "Women's Lives Viewed from an Evolutionary Perspective II. Patterns of Helping." 6 *Ethology & Sociobiology* 155 (1985).

Feigelman, W., and A. Silverman. *Chosen Children: New Patterns of Adoptive Relationships.* 1983.

Fisher, R. *The Genetical Theory of Natural Selection.* 1958.

Flew, A. "From Is to Ought." 1967. Reprinted in *The Sociobiology Debate*, ed. A. Caplan. 1978.

Flinn, M. "Resources, Mating, and Kinship: The Behavioral Ecology of a Trinidadian Village." Ph.D. diss. Northwestern University, 1983.

Fox, R. "Kinship Categories as Natural Categories." In *Evolutionary Biology and Human Social Behavior*, ed. N. Chagnon and W. Irons. 1979.

Freedman, D. *Human Sociobiology: A Holistic Approach.* 1979.

Fruin, J., ed. *De Nederlandse Wetboeken.* 1986.

Gaulin, S., and A. Schlegel. "Paternal Confidence and Paternal Investment: A Cross-Cultural Test of a Sociobiological Hypothesis." 1 *Ethology & Sociobiology* 301 (1980).

Gould, S. J. *Ever Since Darwin: Reflections in Natural History.* 1979.

Grafen, A. "A Geometric View of Relatedness." In *Oxford Surveys in Evolutionary Biology*, vol. 2, ed. R. Dawkins and M. Ridley. 1985.

Haimes, E., and N. Timms. *Adoption, Identity and Social Policy: The Search for Distant Relatives.* 1985.

Hames, R. "Relatedness and Interaction Among the Ye'kwana: A Preliminary Analysis." In *Evolutionary Biology and Human Social Behavior*, ed. N. Chagnon and W. Irons. 1979.

Hamilton, W. D. "The Evolution of Altruistic Behavior." 97 *Am. Naturalist* 354 (1963).

———. "The Genetical Evolution of Social Behavior, I & II." 7 *J. Theoret. Biol.* 1 (1964).

Havighurst, H. "Services in the Home—A Study of Contracts Concepts in Domestic Relations." 41 *Yale L. J.* 386 (1932).

Hirshleifer, J. "Privacy: Its Origin, Function, and Future." 9 *J. Legal Stud.* 649 (1980).

House Armed Services Committee. *The All-Volunteer Force and the End of the Draft.* Reprinted in *House Armed Services Committee Hearing*, Comm. Ser. no. 93-9, at 427, 428 (Apr. 10, 1973).

Hrdy, S. B. *The Woman that Never Evolved.* 1981.

Irons, W. "Kinship." In *Evolutionary Biology and Human Social Behavior*, ed. N. Chagnon and W. Irons. 1979.

———. "Why Lineage Exogamy?" In *Natural Selection and Social Behavior*, ed. R. Alexander and D. Tinkle. 1981.

———. "Human Female Reproductive Strategies." In *Female Social Strategies*, ed. S. Wasser. 1983.

Jewell, M. *The State Legislature: Politics and Practice.* 1969.

Katz, S. Introduction to J. Triseliotis, *In Search of Origins.* 1973.

Kitchen, W. *Federal District Judges: An Analysis of Judicial Perceptions.* 1978.

Kitcher, P. *Vaulting Ambition: Sociobiology and the Quest for Human Nature.* 1985.

Klibanoff, E. "Genealogical Information in Adoption: The Adoptee's Quest and the Law." 11 *Fam. L. Q.* 185 (1977).

Konner, M. *The Tangled Wing: Biological Constraints on the Human Spirit.* 1982.

Krause, H. *Family Law Cases and Materials.* 1976.

————. *Child Support in America: The Legal Perspective.* 1981.

Kurland, J. "Paternity, Mother's Brother, and Human Sociality." In *Evolutionary Biology and Human Social Behavior,* ed. N. Chagnon and W. Irons. 1979.

Leibson, D. "Recovery of Damages for Emotional Distress Caused by Physical Injury to Another." 15 *J. Fam. L.* 163 (1976–77).

Lenington, S. "Child Abuse: The Limits of Sociobiology." 2 *Ethology & Sociobiology* 17 (1981).

Lewontin, R., S. Rose, and L. Kamin. *Not in Our Genes.* 1984.

Lieberman, J. *Child Support in America: Practical Advice for Negotiating—and Collecting—a Fair Settlement.* 1986.

Lightcap, J., J. Kurland, and R. Burgess. "Child Abuse: A Test of Some Predictions from Sociobiological Theory." 3 *Ethology & Sociobiology* 61 (1982).

Littlefield, C., and J. Rushton. "When a Child Dies: The Sociobiology of Bereavement," 51 *J. Personality and Soc. Psychology* 797 (1986).

Lockard, J. "Speculations on the Adaptive Significance of Self-Deception." In *The Evolution of Human Social Behavior,* ed. J. Lockard. 1980.

Lopreato, J. *Human Nature and Biocultural Evolution.* 1984.

Lumsden, C. J., and E. O. Wilson. "Translation of Epigenetic Rules of Behavior into Ethnographic Patterns." 77 *Proc. Nat'l Acad. Sci.* 4382 (1980).

————. *Genes, Mind, Culture: The Coevolutionary Process.* 1981.

————. *Promethean Fire: Reflections on the Origin of Mind.* 1983.

Markham, E., B. Lindsey, and G. Creel. *Children in Bondage.* 1914. Reprint, 1969.

Masters, R. "Is Sociobiology Reactionary? The Political Implications of Inclusive-Fitness Theory." 57 *Q. Rev. Biology* 275 (1982).

Matthews, D. *U.S. Senators and Their World.* 1960.

Maxwell, M. *Human Evolution: A Philosophical Anthropology.* 1984.

McCormick, C. *McCormick on Evidence.* 1984.

Midgley, M. "Gene Juggling." 1979. Reprinted in *Sociobiology Examined,* ed. A. Montagu. 1980.

Montagu, A. Introduction to *Sociobiology Examined.* 1980.

————, ed. *Sociobiology Examined.* 1980.

Morris, R. *Evolution and Human Nature.* 1984.

Murphy, J. *Evolution, Morality, and the Meaning of Life.* 1982.

Northwestern University Law Review Board of Editors. "Breaking the Seal: Constitutional and Statutory Approaches to Adult Adoptees' Right to Identity." 75 *Nw. U.L. Rev.* 3116 (1980).

Note, "Domestic Relations—the Presumption of Gratuitous Services—Must a Wife Work for Free?" 16 Wake Forest L. Rev. 235 (1980).

Oakley, J. "Sociobiology and the Law." In *Man, Law and Modern Forms of Life,* ed. E. Bulygin, et al. 1985.

O'Sullivan, J., and A. Meckler. *The Draft and Its Enemies.* 1974.

Parmiter, G. *The King's Great Matter: A Study of Anglo-Papal Relations 1527-1534.* 1967.

Perkins, R., and R. Boyce. *Criminal Law* (3d ed.). 1982.

Pfeiffer, J. *The Emergence of Society.* 1977.

Pierce, W. L. "Survey of State Laws and Legislation on Access to Adoption Records—1983." 10 *Fam. L. Rep.* 3035 (1984).

Pitlo, A. *Het Nederlandse Burgerlijk Wetboecken.* 1981.

Posner, R. *The Economics of Justice.* 1983.

Prosser, W. *Law of Torts.* 1971.

Quinton, A. "Ethics and the Theory of Evolution." 1966. Reprinted in *The Sociobiology Debate,* ed. A. Caplan. 1978.

Rawls, J. *A Theory of Justice.* 1971.

Rodgers, W. "Bringing People Back: Toward a Comprehensive Theory of Taking in Natural Resources Law." 10 *Ecology L. Q.* 205 (1982).

Rosenthal, A. "The State of State Legislatures: An Overview." 11 *Hofstra L. Rev.* 1185 (1983).

Ruse, M. *Sociobiology: Sense or Nonsense.* 1979.

————. *Taking Darwin Seriously: A Naturalistic Approach to Philosophy.* 1986.

————, and E. Wilson. "Moral Philosophy as Applied Science." 61 *Philosophy* 173 (1986).

Russell, R., and P. Wells. "Estimating Paternity Confidence." 8 *Ethology & Sociobiology* 215 (1987).

Ryan, J., A. Ashman, B. Sales, and S. Shane-DuBow. *American Trial Judges: Their Work Styles and Performance.* 1980.

Sahlins, M. *The Use and Abuse of Biology: An Anthropological Critique of Sociobiology.* 1976.

Schatkin, S. *Disputed Paternity Proceedings* (4th rev. ed.). 1975.

Schwartz, R. "On the Prospects of Using Sociobiology in Shaping Laws: A Cautionary Note." In *Law, Biology and Culture,* ed. M. Gruter & P. Bohannan. 1983.

Seemanova, E. "A Study of Children of Incestuous Matings." 21 *Human Heredity* 108 (1971).

Seymour, F., C. Duffy, and A. Koerner. "A Case of Fertility in a Man, Aged 94." 105 *J.A.M.A.* 1423 (1935).

Sheehan, T. "Paris: Moses and Polytheism." 1980. Reprinted in *Sociobiology Examined,* ed. A. Montagu. 1980.

Shepher, J. "Mate Selection among Second Generation Kibbutz Adolescents and Adults: Incest Avoidance and Negative Imprinting." 1 *Archives Sexual Behavior* 293 (1971).

————. *Incest: A Biosocial View.* 1983.

Simons, A. "Psychic Injury and the Bystander: The Transcontinental Dispute between California and New York." 51 *St. John's L. Rev.* (1976).

Singer, P. *The Expanding Circle.* 1981.

Smith, M., J. Kish, and C. Crawford. "Inheritance of Wealth as Human Kin Investment." 8 *Ethology & Sociobiology* 171 (1987).

Sociobiology Study Group of Science for the People. "Sociobiology—Another Biological Determinism." 1976. Reprinted in *The Sociobiology Debate,* ed. A. Caplan. 1978.

Sorenson, A., and M. MacDonald. "An Analysis of Child-Support Transfers." In *The Parental Child-Support Obligation,* ed. J. Cassetty. 1983.

Sorosky, A., A. Baran, and R. Pannor. "The Effects of the Sealed Record in Adoption." 133 *Am. J. Psychiatry* 900 (1976).

―――. *The Adoption Triangle*. 1978.

Surrey, S., W. Warren, P. McDaniel, and H. Gutman. *Federal Wealth Transfer Taxation*. 1977.

Sussman, M., J. Cates, and D. Smith. *The Family and Inheritance*. 1970.

Symons, D. *The Evolution of Human Sexuality*. 1979.

Thornhill, R., and N. W. Thornhill. "Human Rape: An Evolutionary Analysis." 4 *Ethology and Sociobiology* 137 (1983).

Trivers, R. "The Evolution of Reciprocal Altruism." 1971. Reprinted in *Readings in Sociobiology*, ed. T. Clutton-Brock & P. Harvey. 1978.

―――. *Social Evolution*. 1985.

Turke, P., and L. Betzig. "Those Who Can Do: Wealth, Status, and Reproductive Success on Ifaluk." 6 *Ethology & Sociobiology* 79 (1985).

van den Berghe, P. *Human Family Systems, An Evolutionary View*. 1979.

―――. "Human Inbreeding Avoidance: Culture in Nature." 6 *Behavioral & Brain Sci.* 91 (1983).

Vernier, C. *American Family Laws*. 1931.

Ward, E., and J. Beuscher. "The Inheritance Process in Wisconsin." 1950 *Wis. L. Rev.* 393.

Webster's Third New International Dictionary of the English Language (unabridged, 1981).

West Eberhard, M. "The Evolution of Social Behavior by Kin Selection." 50 *Q. Rev. Biology* 1 (1975).

Wigmore, J. *Evidence* (Chadbourne rev.). 1970.

Williams, G. C. *Adaptation and Natural Selection*. 1963.

―――, ed. *Group Selection*. 1971.

Williston, S. *Williston on Contracts*. 1957.

Wilson, E. O. *Sociobiology: The New Synthesis*. 1975.

―――. *On Human Nature*. 1978.

―――. *Sociobiology: The Abridged Edition*. 1980.

―――. *Biophilia*. 1984.

Wilson, M. "Impact of the Uncertainty of Paternity on Family Law." 45 *U. Of Toronto Fac. L. Rev.* 216 (1987).

Wolf, A., and C. Huang. *Marriage and Adoption in China, 1845–1945*. 1980.

Wrangham, R. "Mutualism, Kinship and Social Evolution." In *Current Problems in Sociobiology*, ed. King's College Sociobiology Group, Cambridge. 1982.

Index

Note on the Author

John H. Beckstrom is a professor of law at Northwestern University Law School. He received his J.D. from the University of Iowa, graduating magna cum laude. He received his LL.M. from Harvard and an M.A. in African studies from the University of London, where he served as a Fulbright Postdoctoral Fellow. Under two Ford Foundation grants (1969 and 1971) Beckstrom led research teams in Ethiopia that reported on that country's legal system and society. His articles have appeared in a variety of law reviews and other scholarly journals. Beckstrom's previous book was entitled *Sociobiology and the Law: The Biology of Altruism in the Courtroom of the Future* (1985).